Matt, Melford, Miracles: A Boy's Courageous Journey

by

Maureen Wierman

DORRANCE
PUBLISHING CO
EST. 1920
PITTSBURGH, PENNSYLVANIA 15238

Dorrance Publishing Co
585 Alpha Drive
Suite 103
Pittsburgh, PA 15238
Visit our website at *www.dorrancebookstore.com*

ISBN: 978-1-6480-4094-8
eISBN: 978-1-6480-4918-7

Dedication

Dedicated to my incredible husband Rich whose steadfast love carried me through this journey as we walked through it together, and to our daughters, Aimee and Kristy, whose perseverance and strength taught me so much about what it means to be a family during times of crisis.

Preface

"I took courage, for the hand of the Lord my God
was on me." Ezra 7:28b

In 1987, our son Matt died. He was eight years old.

It has been a thirty-year process to get this book from my mind and heart onto the printed page. I am frustrated that it took me so long, but I've learned that grief is a lifelong process. And that I am still on my grief journey, still learning what grief looks like and what it feels like.

I have several purposes in writing this book. First, I want to honor Matt's legacy. It has always been crucial for me as Matt's mom that he is not forgotten. This book is my promise to Matt—that his life would be remembered.

I also want to honor my husband, Rich, and our two incredible daughters, Aimee and Kristy. It has only been recently that I have learned the impact this loss has had on their lives. The pain that they have endured, the courage with which they have moved forward, is testimony to their strength as individuals. The impact of grief on a marriage has been a difficult and powerful experience. Without the love and presence of the Lord in our marriage, we may have become a statistic that is too prevalent among couples that lose a child. Rich's ongoing love and his always trying to understand my grief is a gift to me.

Writing Matt's story has been healing for me. I want it to be encouraging and helpful to you, my reader. And that leads me to the most important reason I wrote this book. It is to let you know that God is trustworthy and sovereign. He loves us and is present throughout all the experiences of our lives. I know that without Him I would not have come through this journey whole. I know it probably would have destroyed me, my family, and those closest to us.

God was and is my strength and peace, and more importantly, He was Matt's peace. Throughout his short life, Matt's actions and responses proved that he had God's peace. To me, this was both comforting and miraculous.

As you follow Matt's story in this book, my prayer is that you can see, as I have learned, that God's hand is on every event, from beginning to end. During this journey, I'm not sure I always saw His hand, but looking back, I can truthfully say that His hand was on not only Matt, but on our whole family.

Acknowledgments

"Oh give thanks to the Lord for he is good; for his steadfast love endures forever." Psalm 118:1

The visitors:

Make-A-Wish: A wonderful couple came by to deliver Matt's three wishes. Make-A-Wish had already sent our whole family to Disneyland, mentioned later. When we were admitted to the bone marrow transplant unit, once again this wonderful organization appeared.

Matt's wishes were to have a racetrack and to meet a Mariner. On this day they were delivering his wonderful electric racetrack. A few weeks later, we received word that Mark Langston was coming to visit Matt. Mark was the award-winning pitcher for the Seattle Mariners baseball team. Matt loved baseball. He had hoped to meet Alvin Davis, as that was his favorite player. However, once we pulled out the statistics on Mark, Matt was very excited. One afternoon, Mark arrived with his agent and nine-month-old daughter. They waited outside while Mark came to see Matt. He was handsome, friendly, and most of all he was focused on Matt. I would try to ask questions and keep the conversation going, but Mark politely redirected all of the conversation to my son.

This may not seem too unusual to the average person, but one had to realize that Matt's appearance was anything but normal. He had a cortisol reaction to the stress of the hospital or the effects of the treatment and his cheeks and head were large and his features almost grotesque. I was blinded to how terrible he looked but now as I look back at the pictures, I'm taken aback. Mark didn't even seem to notice—he just talked to Matt about baseball, about Alvin Davis (his best friend and roommate), and Matt just beamed. He invited Matt to come to a game anytime. He made a difference in Matt's life and brought a little joy to a very ill and frightened little boy. I was later to learn that Matt was a Christian—he will be forever in my gratitude.

Dave Krieg—the Seattle Seahawks quarterback:
Also, one of my most embarrassing moments. The Seahawks came to the floor to visit the kids and patients. Dave walked into Matt's room just as I was bemoaning the fact (out loud) that he was not doing a very good job this season. Dave apparently didn't hear (I hope) and proceeded to, once again, focus on my son. Okay, so it wasn't a Mariner, but it was someone who took the time to brighten our son's day. Years later, I was asked to teach a private childbirth class to Dave and his wife—and I hope I expressed my gratitude to him then.

Friends and family:
Where do I begin? I remember a very pregnant Evie, my dear friend and long-term roommate in college, coming to see Matt on her break. She worked in the pharmacy at Swedish Hospital, where Matt had his transplant, and would often stop by to say hi.

My dear and long-term friend Ellyn, who would stop by and give me moral support, prayer support, hug support, and any support she perceived I needed but couldn't express. Near the end of Matt's journey, she accompanied me to a clinic appointment with Matt, when his faithful puppet, Melford, "bit" the radio knob off of our car. We laughed so hard we actually cried, Matt included. She is also the one who left a precious note on our car windshield (we didn't even know she had come) on the morning of Matt's surgery, where we learned his cancer had returned: It simply said: "Our God Reigns!!!"

I still have that note and the reassurance it still provides today. He does and He did!!

Mike and Donna, Rich's brother (my brother, too), and his wife—see the story of our Christmas decorations. Mike offered to spend the night so that Rich and I could go home together. We had not been home overnight together since Matt entered Swedish—we were at almost 50 days. The next day we were to learn that Matt spiked a fever that night and Mike was up with him and the nurses almost all night, and the patient next door had "coded," meaning that his heart had stopped and the emergency team had been called. Mike was so gracious and just took it in stride. I'm not sure that I could have done the same.

Jim and Gail Groenink—one of our pastors and his wife—where do I begin? They had three children and Gail was pregnant with their fourth. They were with us all through initial diagnosis and treatment at Children's and now here at Swedish. They had reached out to another patient, Aaron, and his mother, who were from Michigan and had begun attending our church while Aaron was in the hospital. A quiet, but faithful source of prayer, spiritual strength, and encouragement.

Kathy Madson—words aren't sufficient to begin to describe what she did for our family. For nine months, all during Matt's illness, Kathy organized meals so that I really didn't cook for those nine months. She coordinated the meals, who would bring what, pick up dishes, and let people know where we would be. She also included what the girls liked, and much more behind the scenes we will never know. She also had a family of three kids. Laura, her nine-year-old daughter, was one of Aimee's dearest friends at church. Kathy also appeared at the hospital over and over again, bringing food, gifts, and messages. Her untiring love and service overwhelmed us.

The cook at 10SW—Because of the nature of our patients, we had our own cook on our floor. He would cook whatever the patients wanted. It usually wasn't much, because during chemotherapy and radiation, and even after, no one really wanted to eat. The chemotherapy and radiation often caused the food to taste metallic. . The mucositis made it too hard to eat anything at all. One day we told him that Matt wasn't really hungry. He asked us, "Is there anything that sounds good to him?" Matt brightened and said a soft taco from Taco Time sounded good. This was from a boy who really hadn't eaten in weeks. He had IV fluids and hyperalimentation to supply his nutritional needs intravenously. Our chef ran to Taco Time about a mile from the hospital, and brought Matt his taco. Our hearts were so full of gratitude. He didn't have to do that.

It was my sister, Marta, who gave Matt Melford, the infamous puppet. We weren't sure what he was—a dinosaur? He was a lifesaver for Matt—he didn't leave Matt's side. When Matt got mad at the nurses for another interruption or painful treatment, Melford would "bite" the nurses. If he was frustrated with Rich or me or his sisters, Melford always let us know. Melford became the voice for Matt's emotions and feelings that he couldn't express himself. I'll always be grateful to my sister for Melford.

My cousin Pete's wife, Avis—from Wyoming, she sent Matt a card every single day that he was in the hospital. Always funny and silly, they made us stop and laugh for a few moments.

Our nurse, Teresa—She was a young, single nurse who loved the Lord and was assigned to our family. She had a sweet spirit, kind heart, and extreme patience. It seemed to us that she always listened to our concerns, and focused on Matt. Sometimes she would just come and sit on Matt's bed and read him a story. We were to learn that the burnout rate for nurses on the bone marrow transplant floor was about one and a half years. They had a psychologist assigned to the staff to help them get through the work situation. We had other nurses when Teresa had a day off—Sandy and Sandi—both were full of love and care. I know there were others, but they are close to my heart.

Strangers—we had many—some good and some well-intentioned, but dangerous. Because the patients had little or no immune system, the flow of visitors in the rooms was supposed to be restricted. We had to wear masks in Matt's room and he had to wear one in the hallways. This worked well, albeit sleeping on the cot in Matt's room with a mask on was interesting—I awoke on more than one occasion ripping the mask off as I was dreaming that I was choking. At Christmas, we had Dickens carolers in the halls filling our rooms with Christmas carols. One evening a flautist and hammered dulcimer sat outside our door, entertaining us with beautiful folk music. One frightening evening, a group of three or four well-meaning young people stormed into Matt's room to say hello. I was angry, as I didn't know who they were—and that they couldn't come into Matt's room, as his immune system was so compromised. They were very apologetic, but I was incensed that they had come in unannounced and uninvited, possibly putting our son's life in danger.

Our children's pastor and wife came to visit, and after they left, we found an envelope of $500 cash on the table. They told us over and over it wasn't from them. It was a welcome gift at Christmas.

Our friends Dwayne and Lorelle, whose daughter, Elizabeth, was born right before our Kristy. They came to the hospital many times, just as they were there for all of our children's births. The night before transplant, Kristy, age four, was admitted to the third floor in preparation for her bone marrow donation to her brother. We were on the tenth floor. I felt so torn, as I couldn't be both places at the same time. I remember walking into Kristy's room to say goodnight, and she and Elizabeth had the hospital beds in the highest positions and were jumping as high as they could on the beds, laughing and giggling. I could only picture Kristy falling, and breaking a bone, and transplant having to be delayed. Dwayne reassured me he was there and would be responsible. Kristy was thrilled and it made her evening so much better.

It was Dwayne and Lorelle who kept our girls the night Matt died, and who invited us to sleep there that morning before we drove home. I remember them opening their home, their lives, everything to make our final journey a little easier.

Our neighbors, Steve and Laurie—who provided us a Thanksgiving banquet, carried all the way from home and set up in the family room. It was wonderful and made it feel like Thanksgiving.

Our friends Joe and Linda Sloss, and their son, John—they brought New Year's Eve to the family room for all of the families on the tenth floor. We had treats of every kind and Matt had one of his best friends to visit. Little did we know that would be the day the doctors would call us to the conference to tell us that the transplant had failed and the leukemic cells were once again growing in Matt's body.

There were so many more friends and family and people behind the scenes that I can't even recall, because I probably will never know how many people reached out and helped us and our family. One feels so helpless, as the human reaction is "How can I ever pay these wonderful people back?" We soon learned that you don't pay them back, for it is out of the depths of their hearts that they were looking for ways to help. We learned this one day when our friend Todd, three doors down, relapsed during transplant. His young wife was sitting outside his room in the Intensive Care Unit (ICU), and Rich went there to see her. He kept asking, "What can I do? How can I help?" Susan kept shaking her head, saying, "Nothing, I'm fine." Finally, she looked up at Rich and sheepishly asked for a glass of milk. Rich raced down the hall to the family room and poured a glass of milk, feeling like it was gold. He told me that his heart was so full, because he could do something to help. That changed our attitude completely—we had to learn to accept the help graciously and gratefully, because it also helped the givers who were desperately trying to make us feel better.

Always I look back on our daughters, whose lives were thrown into chaos from the moment of diagnosis. Aimee was nine and Kristy was four, and their lives were forever changed. I tried so hard to not let them be left behind or ignored. Honestly, there were times that the moments were so intense; I'm not sure how they got from here to there. If not for dear family and friends, picking them up from school and getting them to activities, their experience might have been much more difficult. So many friends would bring gifts for Matt, and then remember the girls and have gifts for them, too. Linda Sloss and Carol Kampman, dear friends who often picked up Kristy from preschool, were such a gift to us. Kristy looked so forward to these times. I can still hear her calling for Carol Kampman!! Kathy Madson had Aimee over so often and gave her joyful, fun times and family ties that we couldn't provide. All the friends and family not only poured into our lives as parents, but also in to the lives of all three of our children, and each in their own way provided a gift of "normalcy" in a time that was anything but normal.

Most importantly, the constant presence of our Lord. He made His presence known in so many ways. In the daily miracles we saw and didn't expect. In the people in our lives mentioned above, and I know there are so many more I didn't mention and even some I didn't know that worked to love and support us. We could tell the difference on the floor of the patients who knew the Lord and those who did not. It was dramatic and real. We had hope because of Him.

We knew He was in control, even though we felt out of control. He provided us peace, and though we weren't perfect in trusting Him, we knew we could always come to Him. We also had the hope of seeing our loved ones again, no matter the outcome. Heaven became very real to us on that floor. Oftentimes at night, when Matt was asleep, I'd pull out my bible and God would provide the perfect verse to comfort or encourage me. When I came to the end of myself and my endurance, He was there. He provided very real strength and peace that were neither normal nor human. Hope was our ever-present companion.

I am forever changed in my relationship with God. I struggle in my human self, but always am reminded by Him of His love and presence. I've seen the reality of that on a moment by moment basis both in my own experience, but also in how Matt walked this journey.

Introduction

"Fear not for I am with you; be not dismayed for I
am your God; I will strengthen you, I will help you,
I will uphold you with my righteous right hand."
Isaiah 41:10

Even though I did not always realize it, it is apparent to me now that the hand of God has been on my entire life, shaping the events that would make me the person I am today.

I grew up in a family that handled challenges by being silent. Differences were stifled, not discussed. When you were mad at someone, you just didn't talk to them for weeks at a time. When my parents argued, my mom would go to her room and she and Daddy wouldn't speak to each other for weeks at a time. I learned from them that it was never okay to express anger, a lesson I learned so well that it took many years to learn how to address differences effectively in my marriage without fear of loss or repercussion.

The summer before third grade, my mom took my five-year-old sister and me on a three-week vacation to visit relatives. It was unusual to be gone for so long; we had never done that before. We had a wonderful visit with favorite aunts and uncles. When we got home, I went to my room, and there sitting on my dresser was a note from Dad. It said, "I love you, but I can't live with you." Sitting beside the note was his wedding ring. I didn't know what it all meant, only that my dad wasn't there anymore. I don't remember even talking to my mom or sister about it. I wasn't terrified or scared. I just accepted it. And so I found myself in a single-parent family at a time when divorce was not common.

Fear was a dominant factor in my family, growing up during the Cold War 1950s. Any loud, explosive sound meant to my mom that an atomic bomb had detonated and it was the end of the world. I also had an ongoing fear of getting leukemia. I'm not sure why or where it came from. I don't recall a friend who had leukemia or reading a book or watching a television show about it. I do know that the fear would follow me into adulthood.

To combat these fears, I began looking more and more to God. He drew me to Himself, and when I was 18 years old, I came to know Christ as my personal Savior and my life was changed forever. I had grown up believing in God but it wasn't until that day I knew I had a personal relationship with Christ. I could take my fears to Him instead of trying to handle them all by myself or hoping they would just go away.

My decision to enter nursing school also had a part in my journey. When I entered nursing school, I refused to care for kids with cancer, probably related to my fear of leukemia. One of my early patients, a young father, was diagnosed with Acute Lymphocytic Leukemia (ALL). We spent a lot of time talking about what he wanted to do before he died and how he approached death with a very practical and matter-of-fact attitude. I was taken aback, but curious. As a young twenty-something, death wasn't something I really thought about. It was something I avoided. Don't all twentysomethings feel a bit immortal?

Rich and I met on an 18-hour bus trip to California with the University of Washington Husky Marching Band. He was so worldly to me—he had been to San Francisco before and knew so much about life in general. I was intrigued. Besides, he had adorable long hair and sideburns. Our first date was in San Francisco and was fun, except for the fact he invited two other buddies to go with him! When we returned to Seattle, he asked me out every night for the next week. By the end of the month, near Thanksgiving, we knew we were in love and wanted to get married. Our wedding occurred in August of 1973, a year and a half after we met. Rich was 20 and I was 22. We were both still in college and broke as church mice. Our honeymoon was a three-week camping trip up and down the West Coast. We lived in a murphy bed apartment and commuted by bike to school each day. We were so happy, and didn't even realize we were broke, because we had so much hope in the future, and what it held for us. I was a city girl and he was a farm boy—we were so opposite, we found we complemented each other wonderfully.

By November of 1973, Rich was finishing up his bachelor's degree and I was in graduate school. We had planned a backpacking trip throughout Europe to celebrate our graduations that summer. When I learned that I was pregnant, we cancelled our travel plans, Rich committed to a job, and we began plans to be parents. I started spotting at sixteen weeks of pregnancy, and my doctor told me I would probably miscarry. Four weeks later, I did, and ended up in the hospital for a D&C. I was devastated.

My dad, who had recently reappeared in my life, came to visit me. I was totally surprised, as it wasn't like him to just show up. He seemed quiet and grief-stricken. I appreciated his presence, but was curious as to why it affected him so much.

As we talked, my doctor entered the room to give me the results of my D&C, which he did in the most inappropriate manner. He was personally *excited* because it had been a Hydatid Mole, a condition in which after fertilization a mass of cells is formed instead of a baby. How could he be excited when I'd just suffered a miscarriage? Did he have no compassion for what I was feeling? My whole life had changed with the miscarriage—Rich and I had changed our plans based on having this baby. This was to be our first child, something that we were anticipating with joy. Anger surged within me and I was appalled and furious with his words and his response.

Then the other questions began to arise. So, I asked myself, had it even been a baby at all? Couldn't I even carry a normal baby? What's wrong with me? Will I ever be able to get pregnant again? I felt abnormal and inadequate. Adding to the news that it wasn't even a real baby, the fact that I was twenty weeks pregnant at the time of the miscarriage meant that my chances of choriocarcinoma, a rare cancer, were much higher. For a year, I was followed with tests to make sure I didn't have cancer. The test results were all normal, but once again my fear of cancer grew. Now, it had personally touched my life.

An added part of the journey was that I had miscarried in June, and Rich was to start his first engineering job in July. We moved from Seattle to Eastern Washington and Rich began his career. One July morning, my dad called to tell me he was going into the hospital for some tests, and he started crying. I asked him if he wanted Rich and me to come, but he said no, he would be all right. That was the last time I spoke with my dad. A few days later, my mom would call to let me know he was in a hepatic coma and not expected to live much longer. Rich and I made a flying trip to Seattle. I remembered what I had learned, that even in a coma a person can still hear. So, I leaned down to my dear father and whispered in his ear, "Daddy, I love you." He died a short time later.

Now I understood why my father had come to the hospital and was so quiet after my miscarriage. I believe he knew he was dying and would never see his grandchild. My first experience with death and grief had happened. This was not how life was supposed to happen.

But God had a plan, and I kept on the journey of learning day by day to walk with Him and to know that He is sovereign over my life.

Later, during Matt's journey, God gave me a verse that I continue to hold on to and I share it now as it became a theme of Matt's story:

"The eternal God is your refuge, and underneath are the everlasting arms." (NIV) Deuteronomy 33:27

Chapter 1

Beginnings

"Behold, children are a gift from the Lord."
Psalm 127:3 (NIV)

It was the coldest day of the year, and I was a week past my due date, when I was awakened by strong contractions. "Oh, no," I moaned to my husband lying next to me. "I'm too tired to have a baby today." With those words, the entrance of Matthew Lyall Wierman into the world began.

We hurried outside to get in the car, leaving our almost two-year-old daughter, Aimee, with her grandma and two dear friends, who were visiting from Seattle. As Rich hurried to start our "dependable" car, our brand-new Datsun pickup, he discovered that the battery was dead. Our less dependable Opel Kadet station wagon was the only remaining choice. So, he bundled me into the car and headed off to the hospital. No one was on the road. It was 8:30 on New Year's morning, 1979.

About a mile from the hospital, the car's engine just died. As Rich coasted the car over to the curb, I burst into tears and the contractions came faster and more furiously. Rich reassured me that we would be fine, as we had our trusty CB radio—a purchase he had convinced me would be worth the money. However, no one was on their CB on New Year's morning. So, he proceeded to try to flag someone down. The few cars that came by, maybe three in all, would move as far away from Rich as they could and pass us by. I was sure that our baby would be born in the back seat of our little car.

My brave husband then jumped into the middle of the road and boldly stated that the next car would either stop or run him down. The driver of a beat-up old pickup full of junk slowed and pulled over. He was a very kind gentleman who offered to take us to the hospital. He appeared a little shaken by my "breathing away" each contraction!

We arrived at the hospital, only to discover that the pipes had frozen and water was scarce. My doctor walked into my labor room, and his first words were "You had to pick New Year's Day, didn't you?"

Our not-so-little Matt entered the world at 8 pounds, 14 ounces, during halftime of the Rose Bowl football game. (Yes, I did watch the game in between contractions.) Yes, I did manage to slug my husband for having the audacity to fall asleep during my labor. What was he thinking? Not a very auspicious beginning for our son.

Little did we know that this crazy birth story would usher in the sweetest little boy to our family.

Matt entered the world with his eyes squeezed shut! It was as if he was saying, "Please let me go back to where it's safe!" This was the opposite of his older sister, Aimee, who entered the world with her eyes wide open, as if to say, "Hello, world, here I come!" That quiet, reserved attitude in Matt turned out to be the theme of his short but well-lived life.

Matt was sensitive and caring and "all boy." He adored his sister Aimee. They were like twins, only twenty-one months apart, and almost the same size as they grew. He loved and protected his little sister, Kristy, who arrived when Matt was three.

When Matt was an infant, I would frequently yell at the cat to get off the counter, and he would cry. We learned in disciplining Matt, he was very compliant, and we never had to remind him more than once to obey. This was a shock to us as parents after our experience with our first child. Aimee would test us at every step. One time when Rich had to spank her, she said defiantly through gritted teeth, "That didn't hurt!" Where Aimee challenged our authority frequently, Matt quietly obeyed.

This is not to say that he was perfect. Matt and Aimee were always playing, teasing, and wrestling each other. We told Aimee many times, "Be nice to your brother, as he may soon be bigger than you, and he will be able to sit on you." It wasn't long before he was and he did!

Matt and Aimee had a special language. When he was three years old, my mom asked me if I'd considered speech therapy for him. I was dumbfounded! He was fine! When his preschool teacher also recommended it, I knew I needed to follow through. Because Matt and Aimee were so close, Aimee would interpret for him to Rich and me. He never had to correct his speech. Matt was diagnosed with a motor-sequencing disorder, which meant that his brain moved faster than his motor skills could keep up. His speech was pretty much unintelligible. Aimee, however, knew exactly what he was saying, and we relied on her translation. Matt was in speech therapy for two years at the University of Washington and he loved it! We were blessed with wonderful student therapists, who made each session fun. By the time Matt entered kindergarten, he was speaking clearly.

Matt was one to always "test the water" before he jumped in to anything new. He always wanted to make sure it was a safe situation. That reminds me a lot of myself. Cautious, but not afraid, he was always following his sister on many adventures. That's why Rich and I were so surprised when one day at my mom's swimming pool, Matt ran ahead and jumped right in...the deep end! He didn't know how to swim! Our friend Dwayne thankfully was close behind and jumped in after him and pulled a very surprised little boy to safety.

In preschool, Matt was popular and loved his friends. I remember picking him up after school one day, and Matt was insistent on meeting the "boy with the hot air balloon coat." That was the beginning of a wonderful friendship with John Sloss and his parents. John was a friend who stuck by Matt even through his illness, and his parents were a source of strength and help for our whole family.

Matt was also one of those kids at preschool who, if the child next to him acted up, he would also. He was the definition of a follower, not a leader. I worried so much about this, concerned about how he would resist drugs and temptation as a teenager, when he was so easily swayed by other kids.

3

By God's grace, Matt would develop into a strong leader very soon. In first grade, his teacher asked us if it was all right to sit Matt next to a child with behavior problems, because he modeled such good behavior. He had become the leader that everyone looked up to.

Aimee was a gifted student and in first grade was enrolled in the school's Quest program, a special curriculum for highly capable children. When Matt was about to enter first grade, we inquired about Quest for Matt, as he was a strong student. His teacher, in her wisdom, asked us if we would rather have Matt succeed at a high level in a regular classroom, or struggle in a gifted class. Rich and I both agreed that his success was more important than the prestige of Quest. Matt really couldn't care—he had so many friends in his class and was more focused on them and baseball than school.

As his little sister Kristy grew, Matt took on the role of her protector. He took his role seriously and wouldn't let her walk too close to the street and constantly nagged her to get away from the curb. Kristy looked up to him and wanted to be just like him. Matt's patience would often wear thin, as Kristy was persistent in her desire to be included. Even so, he loved her and watched over her. God's hand was on them both, as later Kristy would be chosen to be his bone marrow donor.

Matt loved animals—we had hamsters, cats, fish, rabbits, and our dog, Tony. He and Matt had a special relationship. Matt's sensitive spirit and gentle ways were perfect for our dog. In Matt's predictable style, he cared for and worried about Tony constantly.

We seemed to be a perfectly normal family of five. Our lives were full of kids' activities, school, carpools, sleepovers, and just trying to keep up. It's hard to discern if I only remember the good times, or if Matt really was an extraordinary little boy. Matt would grow to be sensitive, caring, and compassionate. He was a truly loving brother to his two sisters.

Rich and I loved watching how our children's relationships grew and developed as they got older. God blessed us with Aimee, Matt, and Kristy, and we have always loved each of them fiercely, and with all our hearts.

There is no doubt our love and admiration for our children helped pull us through the excruciating time that lay ahead.

Chapter 2

A Summer Gift

"For as the heavens are higher than the earth,
So are my ways higher than your ways,
And my thoughts than your thoughts."
Isaiah 55:9 (ESV)

The summer of 1986 would prove to be one of the most remarkable summers that our family had experienced. At the start of it, Rich did an amazing thing. I still remember the five of us sitting down together in the living room and planning our summer. Rich started by explaining to our kids that Wednesday nights would be family nights, and nothing would interfere with that. As a mother, I was delighted to live out this priority in real terms. Aimee was nine, Matt was seven, and Kristy was four, and they were full of ideas when their dad explained that each one of them would contribute ideas as to what they wanted to do on those important nights.

Each child offered several ideas on how they'd like to spend Family Night. They came up with many suggestions, ranging from the rides at the Seattle Center, to camping, to going for ice cream, to movies, or to a baseball game. As each suggestion was made, Rich would write them down and we then posted the list on our refrigerator for the summer. The list grew with almost daily additions from the kids, as did their anticipation.

We built so many memories as a family on those Wednesday nights. I will always be grateful for that exceptional summer, not realizing then how important those memories would become, until one year later, when such experiences together would no longer be possible. Once again, God's hand was on Rich for creating our Family Nights and making memories that I continue to treasure in my heart.

One specific memory that Rich and I both have is going to the Seattle Center's "Funland," where there were attractions of all types—children's boat rides, bumper cars, a roller-coaster, and the scary rides that Aimee and Rich really liked! As we were walking around the center, we spotted a little boy with his family. He stood out to us because he wore a baseball cap to cover his bald head, and a mask for a reason unknown to us. Later that year, after Matt was diagnosed and wore that same "uniform" of a kid with cancer, that picture came back vividly. It was as if God had given us a glimpse of what was coming. It wasn't a surprise—it was familiar. We had seen it before!

God was to provide me with many unique events that would prepare and reassure me as we entered Matt's journey with cancer. As a Christian family, our faith plays a central and critical role in our lives. As a mom, I had asked God to allow me to lead all of our children to Christ. It was enormously important for me and was my central prayer for my children. God granted me that desire, and by the time each of them had turned five, I had the privilege and gift of leading them to the Lord.

So, it was startling that summer when seven-year-old Matt, as I was putting him to bed, asked if he could ask Jesus into his heart. I reminded him that he had already done that and you only need to do that once and He would live there forever. Matt insisted, and so we prayed together, and Matt asked the Lord into his heart. This recurred over and over again that summer. Finally, as we were again praying at bedtime, I asked Matt why he continued to ask Jesus into his heart. Matt's reply was straightforward and very Matt-like: "I just want to be sure, Mommy."

Matt's Sunday school teacher assigned a memory verse that summer. Again, it was no accident. Matt would repeat it every night before we prayed.

It was John 3:16:

"For God so loved the world that he gave his only Son, that whoever believes in him should not perish but have eternal life." (ESV)

I can't help but believe that this reassured and encouraged Matt as he demonstrated such peace throughout his whole journey with cancer.

What a precious gift God gave him that summer. And to me!

Also, that summer we joined a Sunday school class called "The Inquirers." It was made up of people of all ages and all walks of life. We were able to know people in our large church on a deep and caring level. Rich and I would soon come to learn how important that seemingly small decision would be in our family's life.

The summer ended all too quickly, and school once again started with the eager anticipation each September brings. New school clothes, school supplies, teachers, and classrooms marked the start of the new school year. Little did we know that three weeks into the year our lives would change forever.

Chapter 3

Diagnosis

"What do I have to dread, what have I to fear,
leaning on the everlasting arms; I have blessed
peace with my Lord so near, leaning on the
everlasting arms." Elisha Hoffman

The 1986 school year started without drama. Aimee was in fourth grade and Matt was in second grade, both at the Peter Kirk Elementary. Kristy started preschool full of excitement. Little did we know what would transpire over the next few weeks.

About three weeks into the school year, the first red flag appeared. I got a call from Matt at school. He was in tears. He wanted me to come pick him up because his chin was burning. This wasn't like him at all, so I hurried down to school and found him in the office, sobbing. I thought maybe he had licked his chin and it had chapped badly, but he denied that. I couldn't see anything that looked like a burn or infection, but I took him home.

The next day I received the same call from school, and again went to school and brought him home. By Friday, he was almost hysterical from the burning sensation, so I made an appointment to take him to see our doctor. Dr. Kraft saw him and prescribed an antibiotic for tonsillitis and sent us home.

On the way home, Matt seemed to be feeling much better, so feeling reassured, we stopped at a mall. I had promised Aimee she could get her ears pierced and this seemed like a good time. As the first ear was pierced, she asked the technician if she could change her mind for the next ear. We all laughed and told her it was up to her. She bravely got the second ear pierced, but I could tell she wasn't feeling well. As we finished up, I asked her why she wanted her ears pierced. Aimee said she felt that she had to, as she'd told all her friends at school that she was getting them pierced.

We walked across the mall to the Hallmark store, and all of a sudden Aimee fainted and started having a grand mal seizure in the middle of the store. I instantly dropped to the floor, turned her to her side, and tried to support her through the seizure. When she recovered, I looked up and everyone in the store had disappeared... including the cashier and Matt. I found Matt hiding behind a card rack. I picked up Aimee, and walked to the seating area in the mall and just sat there. All of a sudden it hit me that no one had offered to help, no one had called 911, and they had all just run away. I was so angry. We left the mall and went to pick up Kristy at preschool. I remember my worry shifting to Aimee, and felt that Matt's tonsillitis at least was being treated. What would be our next step to help Aimee? Little did I know that Aimee's episode would help clarify part of Matt's eventual treatments and the choice of a bone marrow donor.

Monday came and Matt was no better; in fact, he was worse with more burning pain in his chin. Thinking we were on the wrong antibiotic, I called the doctor and we made an appointment to be seen again. This time, a different physician saw him and looked in his throat for what seemed like an extraordinarily long time. Looking at me seriously, she said that the tonsil was very large and brown, and she was concerned that it could be a cancerous tumor. This was the second red flag.

Dr. Cooley reassured me there was only about a 15% chance that the tonsil was cancerous, but wanted to have him seen by a surgeon, as the tonsil needed to come out. We then proceeded down the block to the surgeon's office. The appointment seemed to take forever. I remember distinctly the surgeon taking off Matt's shirt to listen to his lungs and heart, and I saw little petechiae (small red areas containing blood because of localized hemorrhage) all over his chest. Fear rippled through me, as now I knew we were dealing with something very serious. It was another red flag that this was not a routine childhood illness. I asked him what they were and he offered me some offhanded comment that explained nothing. I felt very discounted for my sincere question and concern. The tonsillectomy was scheduled for the next morning at our local hospital and we were sent to the lab to get Matt's pre-op bloodwork.

We were now at the end of a very long day, and multiple doctor's visits. The three kids were cross and tired, and so was I. We just wanted to get home. I was by then also sick with worry that my son was seriously ill and my oldest daughter would need to be seen by a neurologist. To add insult to injury, the surgeon was a seemingly uncaring healthcare professional, with no bedside manner whatsoever. I was near the end of my patience and totally exhausted with worry. I should have turned to God and asked Him for help, but I think I was truly numb and moving mechanically through the steps of what to do next.

Unknown to us, Matt had become dehydrated, so the lab technician had a terrible time getting Matt's blood drawn. That should have been my next red flag.

Now, one more worry was added to the list. Sometimes I think it would be so much easier if I were not a nurse. I began to realize I knew just enough to be dangerous, but not enough to even know the right questions to ask.

At last, we could go home, all of us exhausted and me totally worried. I will never forget Matt acting out as we got out of the car, and I spanked him. It took me a long time to forgive myself for that—spanking him when he was so ill. I later found out he had only 9000 platelets when the normal is 150,000-400,000 for blood clotting. My only thought was *What kind of horrible mother am I?*

The next morning was a gray, rainy Seattle day. Rich had a previously scheduled dental appointment before work, so our plan was that I would take Matt to our local hospital as soon as the surgeon called with the surgery time, and Rich would meet us there. We then experienced the hand of God, the first of many times when He orchestrated events to give us strength and encouragement. For some odd reason, instead of going to work after his dental appointment, Rich decided to come home. This was the first of many miracles we were to experience. Just moments later the surgeon called to report that Matt had some strange pathology in his blood work, and instead of having the tonsillectomy at our local hospital, we needed to take Matt to Seattle Children's Hospital, another red flag. How grateful I was that Rich was there to receive this startling news with me.

As I listened to the doctor, I wrote "leukemia?" on my notes, wanting so badly to ask that doctor if that was what he suspected. But I couldn't. I did ask what it all meant, and he said we needed further evaluation. So, we bundled up a very sick little Matt and made our way to Children's Hospital, a huge facility famous for its exceptional care of children.

As we walked into a very crowded waiting room the receptionist called out to us, "Is this Matt Wierman?" It seemed that she had been watching for us, another red flag. She said we needed to go to the hematology/oncology clinic instead of surgery. By then, my stomach was churning and I was praying constantly. When we got to the hem/onc clinic, the receptionist said, "Are you Matt Wierman?" As we nodded, she said we needed to go to Admitting instead of the clinic. I asked why, and she only replied, "Didn't the doctors tell you?"

No! I was screaming inside.

After ninety minutes of waiting in admitting, we were finally called. Blessedly, Matt had fallen asleep. We learned that this was his defense mechanism in stressful situations. The dear admitting clerk went through all the normal questions. As she was finishing up, I looked on the paper and under "diagnosis" it said: "R/O Leukemia" – "rule out leukemia." My deepest fears were being realized. Suddenly, I was taken back to my deepest childhood fears, except I was supposed to be the one with leukemia, not my precious son.

I asked her if this was the diagnosis. She looked up and me and said, "Didn't the doctors tell you?"

Inside, I am screaming, *Are you kidding? Is she really asking me the same question that we were asked upstairs?* What did they know that they hadn't told us?

I still wonder why this was the way we learned of Matt's diagnosis: reading it on the admission paperwork. Once again, I know just enough to be dangerous. That's not supposed to be the way it is handled. At least, not in my perfect, follow the rules world.

We were taken up to the third floor and from that point on our treatment by the hospital staff was more than caring and considerate—it was exceptional. Matt would need a bone marrow aspiration, an extremely painful procedure. The results would either confirm or deny the leukemia diagnosis. I prayed and prayed that it wasn't leukemia. Not our Matt. Not our child who was so sweet and sensitive and our only son.

My friend and coworker Patty Hall came to sit with me as we awaited Matt's bone marrow aspiration to be completed. She was such a source of strength. I continue to be amazed by friends and family as they just appeared to support us.

Rich left the hospital room to go home to get Aimee and Kristy, but the battery in the car was dead. Another miracle. He appeared in the hospital room just as the medical team entered to give us the news. I'm so thankful to this day that Rich was there. God knew I needed him there. The group of pediatric oncologists entered Matt's room and told us it was indeed ALL—Acute Lymphocytic Leukemia. They would need to wait for further testing to determine the final diagnosis and prognosis. ALL was 90% curable but there were some rare forms of the disease that were also a possibility. We prayed for the 90%-curable leukemia.

Our nurse, Joyce, came in to the room, and we must have looked a little shell-shocked. She said, "Don't borrow trouble, it could be anything." So we clung to her hope. We were forever thankful for her attitude. And yes, we clung to hope.

I don't remember much after that point: Who spent the night? Did both Rich and I? What about our girls? Life stood still at that point. We were both numb and overwhelmed and, as we found to be true throughout the journey, we could only take one moment at a time. We found God, there moment by moment, and each time, we would move on to the next moment.

The next day, Rich and I were told to wait for the final details of the type of leukemia that Matt had. We continued to pray that it would be one of the 90%-curable ALLs. The chances were slim, per the doctors, that it would most likely be a more serious one.

Meanwhile, Matt needed surgery to insert a Hickman line through which he would receive chemotherapy, nutrition, and fluids. We learned that Dr. Hickman himself would put in Matt's line, and we found out that many years earlier he had lost a daughter. He had been on duty in the emergency when she was brought in after an accident. Dr. Hickman had the empathy and compassion we needed.

Jesus was present in Matt's heart and evident in his life all through diagnosis and treatment. We were able to accompany Matt to the surgery suite, and as I bent down to kiss him, I said, "Matt, don't be afraid. Jesus is going with you." Matt just looked up at me from the stretcher, smiled, and said, "I know, Mom." He had such a peace and showed no signs of fear or anxiety. The faith of a child.

The waiting began. All morning and no news. Rich's brother Gary and I went to lunch in the hospital cafeteria, and I remember seeing a little bald boy with a mask playing outside in the park. It seemed like a premonition. I wondered if that was what we were headed for—my little Matt, with a head full of blond curls, destined to be bald and wear a mask?

At last, Matt was brought back to his room, his Hickman line in place. Everything had gone well. I was so thankful to have him back in our presence. I don't believe that having a child go through any surgery is easy for any parent. Repeatedly, the thought kept racing through my mind, "Lord, please let me trade places with him."

All afternoon we continued to wait for more information, and as we waited, our anxieties grew. Did this mean that it was more serious? Why was it taking so long? In the meantime, more and more gifts and balloons were arriving in Matt's room—it was a joy-filled room! Matt was taking it all in stride and enjoying every moment. His best friend, Tim, came and they played for hours on his hospital bed. What a blessing Tim was to Matt.

Finally, the word came that we were to meet with the doctors in the conference room. Little did we know that this meant bad news. We would learn that the good news was always announced in Matt's room. Bad news was announced in a conference room apart from Matt's hearing.

Rich and I went to the conference room and were greeted by somber faces. The emotion of that moment still takes me aback and makes me catch my breath. Matt's leukemia was a very rare form. That was what had taken so long...now it had a name: **Burkitt's Leukemia**. We had never heard of it. Dr. Burkitt had identified it in Africa and originally thought it was related to the Epstein-Barr virus. It grew as fast as hair or skin cells, which explained why Matt had gone from being perfectly healthy one day and seriously ill ten days later. His bone marrow was so packed with leukemic cells, the doctors had difficulty getting a sample during the bone marrow aspiration.

We were told that Burkitt's Leukemia was very rare—only six cases a year in the U.S. The only treatment was a bone marrow transplant—as soon as possible. I remember the doctors crying, yes, crying, as they told us.

What did all of this mean to Matt? Bone marrow transplant was his only option. His two sisters, Rich, and I would be tested to see if there was a match. Time was not on our side. We needed to move swiftly. Chemotherapy was started that evening and we awaited a possible tumor response. That is when the destruction of the tumor is so rapid, the result is a negative response in the body as it tries to deal with the breakdown of those tumor cells. The liver and the kidneys can fail as they are overloaded with tumor cells. Thankfully, Matt did not develop any tumor response.

The doctors looked for tumor activity in his chin, the source of all his pain. None was ever found. One more question for when we get to Heaven.

Matt dealt with the chemotherapy well. The doctors and nurses were wonderful. The doctors spent a long time with us explaining what the plan was: to reduce the cancer cells to a minimum and then treat what was left with the bone marrow transplant. They had hope for the treatment to be successful. I'm not sure how much we retained, but we were thankful that they took the time to give us the information and plan. I learned that for me, personally, as long as I knew the plan, I could deal with each step of the process. It gave me a sense of security when there was a plan. Dealing with the uncertain outcome was a different story. That's where my dependence of the Lord began to grow and be real in my life.

We were overwhelmed with love and the tangible evidence of God's presence through every step. We lived moment to moment, not even day to day. The emotional roller-coaster of good news, then bad news, took its toll on all of us. Life was stripped down to the bare essentials. We depended on friends and family to help care for our girls and their needs. Our hope was to keep their routines as normal as possible. At the same time, we struggled to survive day to day as parents. Matt had procedure after procedure, trying to determine how far the cancer had spread through his organs. Good news one moment and a sigh of relief. Then bad news and grasping for hope that his young body would be able to fight. We clung to God, to His Word, and His sovereignty. Knowing that He was in control gave us peace, because otherwise we were totally out of control.

Chapter 4

The Community of Children's Hospital

"...give thanks in all circumstances; for this is the
will of God in Christ Jesus for you."
1 Thessalonians 5:18 (ESV)

The staff at Children's Hospital told us we needed to be transferred
to the cancer ward. I was adamant that I didn't want to go there.
Denial was so much more comfortable. I didn't want Matt to be
labeled as a "cancer patient." My dear friend Ellyn, after she was
diagnosed with breast cancer, summed it up perfectly: "I refuse to
be defined by cancer."

As much as I protested, the time came when we had to move to
that floor. What I found was incredible support and help from the
staff and other families there. I was humbled. The staff cared for
our whole family, including Aimee and Kristy. The families reached
out to us. We were bonded together by our cancer diagnosis. It felt
like family, like a warm refuge from the storms that were brewing.
The girls went down to the playroom every day and made friends
with the volunteers—college students who gave of their time to
love on our children. They did crafts, read stories, played, and
mostly were loved.

Volunteers came to Matt's room daily, and they seemed to have a special sensitivity and love for these cancer kids—children dealing with issues well beyond their years. We noted that every child was special in their own way. I have always felt that God had specially picked these children to battle this horrific disease. He knew the ones that could handle the battle best. They demonstrated courage, bravery, strength, and amazing faith. Ranging in age from birth to teenagers, they demonstrated trust in the doctors, their parents, and courage to fight whatever the cost.

I thought back to my days in nursing school, when I was criticized for smiling around cancer patients. Our favorite nurse was Lynn, whose smile and laugh were a healing balm to us as cancer families. She smiled and laughed and we were healed. It almost was a confirmation that I was okay.

Aimee and Kristy were amazing sisters. They rolled with the schedule their brother demanded. They were there to support and love him in their own special way. School took its place as second in the scheme of life. The schools understood. Aimee and Matt's school did fundraisers and blood drives. Dear friends took Aimee and Kristy to school, as we remained in the hospital to be with Matt.

Friends and family were overwhelming in their outpouring of love and support. Little did we know that group of loving people in our Sunday School Class would support us and encourage us throughout and beyond Matt's journey. Most of the time they worked behind the scenes with a wonderful couple, Dave and Elisha Parker. They had lost a son to the same cancer four years earlier, when Seth was twelve. They served as a resource to the class to know how best to help and love us, in big and small ways. We are forever indebted and filled with love and gratitude for them and the class.

The junior high girls at church cleaned my house, and sat around with Rich afterwards to listen to Matt's story. Our friend Kathy arranged meals over and over again. Our friend Mindy made Matt special shorts to wear of bright-colored fabrics. Our pastor and his wife, Jim and Gail Groenink, were there every step of the way for us, taking care of any need we had, spiritually, physically, or emotionally.

It was at Children's Hospital that the presents really began to emerge. Matt's room looked like a toy store and he enjoyed every moment. The doctors would come into Matt's room and laughingly comment that his corner of the hospital was lifting off the ground because of all of his balloons.

Our dear friends remembered Aimee and Kristy with gifts and special adventures. Kristy loved Linda Sloss and Carol Kampman, mothers of two of Matt's best friends, John and Jason. They would pick her up after preschool and go to McDonald's over and over again. She loved those Happy Meals!

Aimee's classmates surrounded her with love and care and family and friends made sure she got to sporting and school events. We prayed that she could maintain a sense of normalcy in her life.

Our children were loved when we weren't able to be the parents we wanted to be. They were given "parents" to step in when Rich and I were distracted with treatments and Matt's needs, and our determination to not have Matt be alone at night in the hospital. We took turns spending every other night with Matt in his room. We slept in sleeping chairs provided by the hospital or in cots beside his bed.

As a mother, I struggled with my emotions. People from church brought us meals, but I couldn't eat. All I could think of was Matt. People visited our hospital room, but all I could think was please go and let us have time with our son. I became very self-centered, centered on family, and very protective. Where was my gratitude, my thankful heart? We were overwhelmed by the outpouring of love, but struggling with the emotional and physical exhaustion and we were staggering under the stress.

I longed to have time as a family, just our family. I wanted to focus on Matt and the girls.

Matt responded as a normal seven-year-old. He got cross with his little sister Kristy. She sat too close to him on his bed and talked too much. It broke my heart, as she just longed to be near her beloved brother. He loved to have his friends visit and play normal boy things. Matt and Aimee shared special times and Aimee loved on her brother over and over again. Kristy worshipped her big brother—he could do no wrong in her eyes. She overlooked his impatience with her and just loved him.

Chapter 5

Our New Routine—What Routine?

"Trust in the Lord with all your heart,
And do not lean on your own understanding
In all your ways acknowledge Him,
And He will make your paths straight." Prov. 3:5-6

The days at Children's Hospital became familiar. As much as I had dreaded the "cancer ward," I found such comfort and peace there. We were there with other families that had children of all ages dealing with cancer. We all had the same bags under our eyes, the stress of maintaining some sense of family, and the fear of the unknown. The adversity of the situation bonded us together.

I came upon a "schedule" for the day-to-day survival of our family, demonstrating the care and the support of our family and friends:

Carol K: Pick up Kristy Tuesday morning at 9:15 A.M.
Cheryl: Pick up Aimee at noon and take to Laurie's for Tuesday
Carol: Pick up Kristy Thursday morning for preschool
Cheryl: Pick up Aimee after school on Thursday
Friday: Same as Thursday
Linda: Drive Monday and Tuesday
Sheryl drives Friday
Gary: Pick up Aimee at Gail's in the morning on Monday
Gail: Drive Wednesday and Thursday to take Aimee to school

Gail: Kristy at your house Tuesday morning

Carol: Picks Kristy up at Gail's in the afternoon

As one can surmise, we would not have been able to care for Aimee and Kristy without the help of dear family and friends. Rich and I were at the hospital almost full time with Matt, as well as Rich trying to work three-fourths of the time. We felt so blessed. This was such a real life demonstration of the body of Christ in action.

After about six weeks, we came to the end of this initial round of chemotherapy, and plans were coming together for our upcoming admission to Fred Hutchinson Cancer Research Center, where Matt's bone marrow transplant would be performed.

As the time for Matt's discharge grew nearer, my anxieties grew. I had found so much security and peace within the walls of Children's Hospital, I didn't want to go home. I didn't want to leave the hospital. I doubted my ability to care for Matt's Hickman line, his medication regime, protect him from infection. Fear was overwhelming me. The doctors and nurses kept reminding me that I would have a multitude of support and information before Matt was discharged.

I kept telling myself, "I am a nurse—I should be able to handle this." Then God would gently remind me that I was a mother in this situation first. The nurse in me took a back seat to the mom who wanted her son to be okay, to survive, to thrive. I didn't want to make a mistake that could harm him.

The day came for discharge preparation. Our cancer resource nurse came in and I once again was reminded of how not to treat patients and families. Her whole focus was on her favorite basketball team and the playoffs and how her husband and son were going to the game. Her excitement was sincere, and understandable. However, we were a family in crisis, faced with possibly losing our only son. I needed the reassurance and knowledge that we would be able to care for him at home. I had so many concerns:

What about the lack of platelets? How could I prevent him from falling while he played outside or rough-housed with Aimee? Would he bleed to death?

How did I keep him safe from infection? It could be life-threatening with his lack of immunity caused by the chemotherapy.

How do I change the dressing on his Hickman line using sterile procedure? (I know, I'm supposed to know how to do this as a nurse, but my confidence was shaken.)

I had so many questions and I needed her help to navigate this plan for going home. I was so angry at her, I don't think I even heard half of what she was saying. That made the situation even worse.

At least we were given reams of paperwork and phone numbers to call anytime we had questions or concerns.

Thankfully, Dr. Flowers, one of our favorite pediatric oncology residents who had diagnosed Matt's cancer, came by Matt's room. She sat down in the rocking chair by the window and just listened and then offered her perspective and wisdom. I wanted to hug her—actually, I think I did!

One of the most impactful things she shared with us stayed with me for the whole journey. She said, "I know the doctors told you that Matt's chance of survival with transplant is 25%. However, when it is your child, it's either 0% or 100%. The numbers don't really matter." To me, it was a reminder that the doctors would do their best to help Matt beat this cancer, but it was in God's hands and up to Him.

The morning arrived, bright and sunny. The staff wheeled Matt out in his wheelchair. We drove a little 1986 Toyota minivan, and we literally packed it full. Between the balloons, the presents, the stuffed animals, medical equipment and medications, there was hardly any room for the kids. We laughed and laughed all the way home at the ridiculousness of the situation. That helped.

It seemed like it had been years since we had been home, but the joy in having our whole family under one roof was overwhelming. This was as it should be—our family together. The fears faded some, and yes, I did take good care of Matt, even the dressing changes. He and Aimee rough-housed constantly, even with my reminders to be gentle!

God was good. He helped me to remember to treasure this time together. I truly did store those memories in my heart. We continued to walk this path one moment at a time, totally dependent on Him.

Chapter 6

The Blur of the Weeks Leading Up to Transplant

"The Lord is my strength and my shield;
In Him my heart trusts and I am helped;
My heart exults and with my song,
I give thanks to Him."
Psalm 28:7 (ESV)

The weeks leading up to transplant are a bit of a blur. So many things happened: appointments, more chemotherapy, meetings. I went to Aimee's and Matt's school, Peter Kirk Elementary, to present Matt's story thus far to the PTA group. I remember telling just a short story of his diagnosis and the group offered to do a blood drive. After the meeting, a woman came up to me to let me know she was a five-year survivor of Non-Hodgkin's Lymphoma. I was so encouraged. The doctors were choosing to call Matt's leukemia a Non-Hodgkin's Lymphoma/Leukemia. Hope was such an important part of our journey, and that evening she gave me a good dose of hope. I will be eternally grateful to her. That demonstrated to me in real and tangible ways the power of one person and their encouragement.

Our whole family was able to tour the children's unit of Fred Hutchinson Cancer Research Center, where Matt would stay during his transplant. The alliance of three entities provided a unique community of cancer care in the Seattle area. It eventually would become known as the Seattle Cancer Care Alliance. The three entities, the University of Washington, Children's Hospital, and Fred Hutchinson Cancer Research Center, worked together to provide an excellence of care and resources that are some of the best in the world. Also, Fred Hutchinson only took the hard cases that no one else wanted, like a seven-year-old boy with Burkitt's Leukemia. In 1986 and 1987 each entity provided a specific, albeit coordinated, part of the care provided to each patient. For us and for Matt, at that time, the initial diagnosis and treatment was provided by Children's Hospital. Their goal was to get Matt into remission, no cancer in his body, as quickly as possible. Once that was accomplished, his care would transfer to Fred Hutchinson, where the bone marrow transplant would occur. Fred Hutchinson had two campuses, the largest of which was housed in Swedish Hospital, in Downtown Seattle. Several of the same doctors worked at each institution, so the continuity of care, so important for the patient and family, was accomplished.

We were able to tour both the Hutch center and the 10SW floor at Swedish Hospital, the two Fred Hutchinson facilities. Matt would be assigned to the Swedish Hospital unit. I was so thankful as that floor was specific for children. My dear friend, Mary Schubert, a nurse practitioner at the clinic where I'd been working, also worked one day a week in the long-term follow-up clinic, caring for women who had been through a bone marrow transplant. She met us there and led us on the tour. Emotions were so mixed that day, both encouragement that the 10SW unit was for children and similar to Children's Hospital in many ways, but also anxious, as we saw the patient rooms on the floor. Outside each room was a picture of the patient before transplant. So full of life and hope, and with hair.

After visiting the units, we hoped that Matt would be chosen for the normal room, not the Laminar Air Floor (LAF) room. In the LAF room there was almost no physical contact. In there, Matt would be in a "bubble"—like a plastic room with people touching him only with gloves through openings in the bubble. It sounded dreadful to me as a mom, with my child not able to experience hugs and physical touch. The policy at the Hutch was to randomly assign patients to one or the other, so it was out of our hands.

The four of us had appointments at Fred Hutch for blood draws to see who was the best match for transplant—Rich, Aimee, Kristy, or me. There were four antigens at that time that needed to match for a transplant to be successful. Fred Hutch was doing transplants on less than perfect matches (4/4) but Matt's chances were better with a perfect match. There would be less chance of rejection or graft vs. host disease, both possible complications after transplant.

I'll always remember the sheer number of tubes of blood they drew from our girls. Aimee and Kristy both handled it so well. That's where we learned of the Red Box. After painful procedures, the kids got to choose something out of the Red Box. It really was pretty amazing—not just "junky toys," as our kids remarked. They had My Little Pony and He-man or Transformers—all among our kids' favorite toys. Both girls were excited and choosing a toy made the procedure much less traumatic. The Red Box became a favorite and important part of the process for the kids.

Then, once again we saw God's hand on and in our lives; Aimee and Kristy were both perfect matches!! The doctors were literally jumping up and down when they gave us the news. They chose little four-year-old Kristy, another of God's provisions. Aimee was our little one who fainted when she got her ears pierced— remember? Kristy was the one that our pediatric dentist chose to model for other three- and four-year-olds, so they could see how brave she was.

Kristy thought the whole procedure would be an adventure— actually, I think she thought of the toys she'd get while in the hospital after seeing her brother's stash. Inside, I think Aimee was a little relieved, even though I know she would do anything to help her brother.

Then, we had to wait. That was one of the hardest parts, because we knew Matt's cancer was a ticking time bomb. Because Burkitt's cancer cells grow so fast, Matt needed to be transplanted as soon as he was in remission. Bone marrow aspirations were done to ensure that all the cancer cells had been destroyed by the chemotherapy. Finally we got the result we had been waiting for: true remission! We knew the best hope for a successful bone marrow transplant was to perform the procedure when the bone marrow was clean with no leukemic cells.

Now, remission had been accomplished, but we had to wait for a bed. We had to wait for the confirmation that we had insurance coverage. That seemed to add insult to injury—we were talking about our son's life. We met many families who had to delay transplant because their initial insurance coverage was declined. It was deemed an experimental procedure at that time. I grew impatient and didn't understand the system and how it worked. In a perfect world, no one would have to wait. I was to learn, in a new way, that God's timing is perfect and I needed to trust Him. My only thought and plea was that it would be soon, for Matt.

Chapter 7

Off to Disneyland!

"Blessed Be Your Name
In the land that is plentiful
Where Your streams of abundance flow
Blessed Be Your Name."
(Lyrics for a song by Mark Redman)

While waiting for admission to Fred Hutchinson Cancer Research Center for transplant, we made many visits to the Children's Hospital Hematology/Oncology clinic. At one such visit, we learned that our neighbors, Laurie and Steve, had contacted the Make-A-Wish organization to arrange for our family to go to Disneyland! We were overjoyed! The kids had never been, and what a bright spot for the kids and something to distract them from the ever-present doctors' visits. Make-A-Wish is a wonderful organization that serves to grant the wishes of critically ill or terminally ill children. They covered all expenses and even provided us with extra spending money. What an answer to prayer for Matt and the whole family.

After speaking with our pediatric oncologist, Dr. Barbara Clark, we seemed to have all the risk areas covered for the trip. She gave us the name of a hospital in Los Angeles if we ran into an emergency. I learned how to cover Matt's Hickman line with a waterproof dressing so he could go swimming—Matt's priority! Whatever anxiety I had about traveling with a son with cancer was overwhelmed with the sheer anticipation of a family trip to Disneyland!!

We scheduled our trip for as soon as possible. Because Matt was in remission, his bone marrow cancer free, the timing was perfect. Off to Disneyland we went!! Rich and I had been there on our honeymoon thirteen years earlier, but not since.

We made the most of every moment. Make-A-Wish had us in a beautiful hotel within walking distance of the park, and with Matt's requisite swimming pool. Joe and Linda Sloss had arranged for us to meet the Disney characters at the entrance to the park in a special way. Kristy found a way to get her picture taken with every character, much to her siblings' chagrin!

We rode the rides, ate way too much junk food, watched the Electric Light parade and the fireworks, chilled at the Haunted Mansion, and screamed on the Matterhorn and Thunder Mountain. Aimee and Matt were very cool in their 3D glasses at the showing of Michael Jackson's Captain EO!

One of my fun memories is asking a Japanese couple to take our picture, and they didn't speak English. They kindly agreed, and looked at our camera, and with a big smile, said, "Ah, Fuji!!" So many ways to communicate!

The evenings were full of miniature golf, swimming, and just enjoying being together as a family. We didn't know what the future held. We had all the emergency plans in place, should Matt spike a fever or run into other health problems. His immune system was still depleted after chemotherapy. I cared for his Hickman line every morning and evening, and covered it with the provided plastic when he went swimming. It was a magical trip and I'm so thankful God provided that period of respite for our whole family.

Our dear friends Steve and Ellyn met us at the airport in Seattle, and as we came off the plane, we must have looked like an advertisement for Disneyland!! Our hats, t-shirts, accessories gave us away! As we headed home, we were decked out in Disney regalia and full of wonderful memories.

Chapter 8
An Unexpected Turn of Events

"When I am afraid,
I will put my trust in You.
In God, whose word I praise,
In God I have put my trust;
I shall not be afraid.
What can mere man do to me?" Psalm 56:3-4

After the wonderful trip to Disneyland, we settled into a false sense of security. The girls were both in school. Matt had his buddies over to play. It seemed like a small sense of normalcy had returned to our family.

However, the anticipation of when Matt could be admitted to Fred Hutch hung over our heads. We prayed for healing and a successful transplant. I prayed nonstop for a bed to become available so Matt could be admitted. The doctors told us it could be weeks.

God had other plans.

We were admitted to the bone marrow transplant unit in a most nontraditional way. My expectation was that we would be admitted in a very systematic and organized manner once the initial workup was completed. Instead, one week after we returned from Disneyland, Matt spiked a fever in the middle of the night. He woke me up, not feeling well, so I checked his temperature. It was 102. I knew that with leukemia and Matt's much-weakened immune system, that could be fatal. I called the doctor on call at Fred Hutch as my directions instructed. He told me to come to Fred Hutch immediately. Almost mechanically, I put Matt in the car and drove the 30 minutes downtown to the hospital. I felt numb and went through the all-too-familiar motions of responding to another possible crisis and threat to Matt's life. Rich stayed at home with the girls, not wanting to disturb them as they slept.

It was after midnight when we parked the car on the street and walked to the smaller Hutch facility that had responded to my call for help. It was not the beautiful hospital we had toured, but an old building that housed some of the transplant patients. I think it was used as a triage unit, where they assessed the patient status and then determined where the patient would go. Capitol Hill, where the hospital is located, is not known to be a safe part of town. When I had worked there as a young nurse, we used to have security guards walk us to our cars for safety. My uneasiness for our safety added to my anxiety over Matt's condition. He seemed his usual peaceful self, not stressed, but quiet as always. He had his Disneyland hat on, his favorite blanket, and was ready to go.

It suddenly hit me that the honeymoon period was over. This was becoming very real. We had experienced an amazing few weeks from remission to this fever, where life seemed almost normal. Now things were once again very unsettled. I reached out to God as we walked, asking for His direction and His peace. I was feeling the all-too-familiar fear begin to return.

The staff at the Hutch facility was wonderful. They set us right at ease, and calmed my fears. One would think that as a nurse, I would feel comfortable in a clinical setting, but once again, when it's your child, nothing is comfortable. Besides, I knew nothing about oncology and transplants—I was a nurse who cared for mothers and babies, not cancer patients. Those two fields are about as opposite as any two could be.

Matt was admitted for observation overnight. We had hoped to get right into the transplant unit at Swedish, but I was told it would be a ten-day wait, because of bed availability. I longed for Matt to be admitted to the children's unit on 10SW at the hospital. I once again reminded myself that with Burkitt's, time was critical. The more we had to wait, the more likely the remission could end, and once again the cancer cells would grow like wildfire. Now, here we are in a strange setting not knowing what the next step would be. This place had not been the focus of our wonderful tour!

My focus turned to finding the cause of Matt's fever and treating it. With any new symptom, my hope would always go to "It's probably something totally unrelated to cancer." Every time, in my experience, the symptom was related to Matt's cancer.

What happened next is not clear in my memory. I do remember that suddenly, a bed became available at Swedish Hospital on 10SW, the children's bone marrow transplant unit. God had worked another miracle against all odds. That very next morning, in early November 1986, Matt was admitted...not ten days later. Matt's fever had moved up the urgency to get him admitted and our fears were lessened. Matt and I gathered our things and walked—yes, walked—the few blocks to Swedish Hospital, to be admitted to the Pediatric Bone Marrow Transplant Unit, Swedish Hospital, floor 10SW.

We arrived at the unit, and another prayer was answered. Matt was admitted to room 1006, the non-laminar airflow room! Matt would not have to be in the plastic bubble!! We were rejoicing!

Matt's room looked like mission control for NASA. His bed looked like it could launch a rocket ship, judging by the number of controls. Matt had a beautiful view out of his window of Downtown Seattle and Puget Sound, where he could see the ferry boats and all the activity on the water. We put Matt's "before" picture on his door outside of his room, just as we had seen on our tour. Rich and I chose his Little League picture in full uniform. It served as a source of hope for our family—of Matt returning to his normal, healthy self!

In 1986, when a patient was admitted to the transplant floor, there were several protocols available. Because it was still an experimental procedure, the patients were randomly selected for one of the protocols. All the transplant procedures involved total body irradiation (TBI) and lethal doses of chemotherapy. In the 1980s, the goal was to kill off the cancer cells with those two treatments; unfortunately, many healthy cells were killed at the same time.

The treatment would take the patient to the verge of death, with very few blood cells left, whether red, white, or platelets. Then the rescue procedure was the transplant—the infusion of healthy bone marrow into the patient from the donor. The goal was to allow the healthy blood cells to grow and multiply in place of the destroyed leukemic cells. Tiny spicules or small particles of bone marrow are present in the material harvested during the transplant. Once the tiny bone marrow "spicules" are infused into the patient's bone marrow, they know exactly where to go to hopefully begin to multiply and create the healthy blood cells to provide complete and healthy immunity and normal blood cell actions, like clotting, carrying oxygen to the body, and many other important roles. The infusion is like a blood transfusion; it appears to be an IV bag of blood that is hung on a IV pole and infused gradually into the patient. **

As parents, we were torn about how best to help Matt adapt to this new setting. Our desire was to provide Matt with as normal an experience as possible, including the comforts of home and time with his sisters and friends. Rich and I hoped to minimize the medical intrusions to as few as possible. We strove for a balance between the multiple medical procedures, tests, healthcare professionals in and out of his room, an environment that was anything but normal, and meeting the needs of a seven-year-old boy.

Rich and the girls joined us later that day, and brought the important items to make Matt feel at home: his quilt, his beloved puppet, Melford, and important treasures like his Transformers, muscle men, and all his over 200 baseball cards. Melford was a gift from my sister to Matt that he used to act out his anger and frustration when he felt overwhelmed. Melford would "bite" the nurses and lash out against them on more than one occasion. He was an important part of Matt's coping mechanisms during the lengthy hospitalization and numerous procedures.

Because we were approaching the holidays, our sister-in-law, Donna, came and decorated Matt's room for Christmas. Our friends, the Slosses, brought a fully lit and decorated miniature Christmas tree! The doctors would stop by daily to see Matt's room. They remarked that it was joyful! That was our hope.

Each transplant patient was assigned a primary nurse to care for them during their journey, responsible for their overall care. We met Theresa Christensen, who would be with us for the whole fifty days of transplant. We immediately loved her! She was such an important part of our lives, providing us security and loving care to Matt and our whole family. Even though she wasn't there 24/7, we knew she could best support and help us in our questions and concerns, and, most importantly, walk with us through the transplant process, because she knew Matt the best.

Matt soon had a whole team of doctors, residents, nurses, social workers, psychologists, physical and occupational therapists who treated him on 10SW. We grew to know and love each one of them. Dr. Rainer Storb, who had created the bone marrow process and program, was one of his doctors. A dignified, gentle man, he told us the story of starting his research in a basement laboratory, and his parents asking him, "Why don't you be a real doctor, with a clinic and everything?" We thank God he chose this path. Dr. Ed Agura was one of the residents. Dr. Ed, as we knew him, was serious but caring and empathetic. Otero Flowers, one of Matt's pediatric oncologists at Children's, was there, too! It was so good to see her familiar face. Since the doctors all rotated, we had each one for a short time, so we were thankful that her rotation coincided with Matt's admission. She became one of our favorite doctors because of her encouraging words during discharge at Children's: "When it's your child, the percentages don't matter; it's either 0% or 100%." Her words proved to be so true.

As we settled into Matt's room and were oriented to the floor, it was time for the doctors to come in and review Matt's case and the plan for treatment. Dr. Cyrus Hill from Australia was designated to go over the plan with us. His wonderful Australian accent made us relax, and as he introduced himself to Matt and Rich and me, he began a three-hour review of all that would be involved. Matt seemingly slept through the whole process—his normal reaction to stressful situations. At least, we thought he was asleep. After Dr. Hill left, Matt proceeded to ask us a multitude of questions about what was said. Rich and I were shocked! He wasn't asleep! He had been listening the whole time! One of his most stinging questions to Rich and me was "Is leukemia cancer?"

Matt had an uncanny sense about the transplant unit and the procedures that would occur. He seemed to remember from Children's that good news was announced in the patient's room and bad news in the conference room. After a few days on the unit, he asked us, "Mom and Dad, please don't leave my room when the doctors come to see me." It seemed to give him a sense of control; if he could keep us there with him, it would be good news.

Another control issue we discovered was the way in which Matt's bone marrow aspirations were done. There were so many things "done to him" that Matt needed to know he could have a say in how they were done. Bone marrow aspirations were necessary to assess how the cancer was progressing or regressing, so they were a frequent procedure. The procedure is extremely painful, as the doctors "punch" a large bore needle through the tailbone several times in order to withdraw samples of bone marrow. The wonderful physicians at Children's had taught Matt to use Ethyl Chloride Spray to numb the skin before they used lidocaine, a Novocain-like medication to numb the area to be injected. Matt called it "freezy spray." Matt taught the doctors at Swedish how he wanted his bone marrow aspirations done, and they listened.

Matt had a definite order: First the staff would use the "freezy spray." During the procedure, I had learned to get down to Matt's level and talk him through the procedure. Being a long-time Lamaze instructor for natural childbirth, I utilized those breathing techniques. Matt and I would stare at each other eye-to-eye and he would breathe with me as I instructed him. One must realize that most children scream through the entire procedure. We knew—we could hear them down the hall. Matt was calm and the doctors literally brought other staff to observe him and how he dealt with the procedure. Rich was much braver than I. He would watch the bone marrow aspiration. Even though I'm a nurse, I couldn't watch. This was my son and that's different than my patient. Once again, I was a mother first.

Finally, the tests and laboratory results were all completed. It was time to begin the process leading up to day "0," transplant day. These were the days of radiation and chemotherapy that would destroy the leukemic and healthy cells. My heart was heavy as I took Matt into the shower, and saw the multiple scars over his body from the aspirations, his Hickman line, and the leftover signs of all that he had so bravely endured. All I could remember was trying so hard to keep him safe up to this point of his life, to prevent injuries, scars, broken bones.

Now we were embarking on the journey that involved lethal levels of drugs and radiation in hopes of saving his life. I prayed that God would bless our decision and would protect Matt through the process.

**Over the years, thanks to research and improvements in treatments, the process has most likely changed from what is described here. This was the procedure in 1986-1987, and provided the most chance for cure for our son at that time. It is interesting to also note that a pediatric oncologist that we met told me that Burkitt's is now 90% curable. We like to think that what was learned from Matt's transplant and others helped to achieve that wonderful outcome.

Chapter 9

The Days Leading Up to Transplant

"On Christ the solid Rock I stand—all other ground
is sinking sand." (Christian Hymn)

During the next few weeks, Rich and I took turns once again spending the night in the hospital. The days were filled with radiation and chemotherapy and constant monitoring of Matt's response to the treatments. He developed a one-sided paralysis on his face, so that his mouth drooped. The physicians thought it could be a Bell's Palsy, common with a compromised immune system. The fear was that it was a symptom that the cancer had spread to Matt's brain, affecting his cranial nerves. The treatment plan was adjusted to address this new symptom with additional chemotherapy.

Matt was put on a gurney and placed in a radiation-shielded room. It was like a bedroom and he was exposed to high level x-rays. This was called TBI—Total Body Irradiation. The room was large with a machine resembling a large urn at one end. This was the source of the Cobalt 60 that provided the radiation. The plan was to kill off all the cancer cells. As the girls and Rich and I sat outside the room, we could hear the hum of the radiation. Matt slept during most of the treatment, even though they provided him with a TV, where he could watch cartoons. It was an uncanny experience. As was his normal reaction, he met it with total acceptance and moved forward. It seemed as if he just totally trusted the process.

Some of Rich's and my journal entries explain the experience best:

11/15/1986—Maureen
Today is Saturday and Matt began his radiation and high dose chemotherapy early this morning. All five of us went to the linear accelerator to begin the radiation for his cranial nerve involvement. He did so well in that and when we got back to his room, he watched cartoons with Aimee and Kristy. About 11:30 his nurse gave him some Benadryl and he fell asleep. The Ara-C (a chemotherapy drug) was added about noon and so far he's doing well. The nurse said that they will keep him pretty heavily sedated. We are praying for a smooth treatment and that Matt doesn't get too sick or experience any complications. I feel like he's been taken away from us for a time, but know he will be given back.

Aimee and Kristy are here today and I know it's hard on them 'cuz nothing's the same and they're out of their routine and comfort zone. They're really doing well and I'm really proud of them.

11/16/1986—Rich
Matt slept thru 3:45 A.M., went to the bathroom, and said his tummy hurt. Nausea at about 4 A.M. and about every half hour since. More Benadryl and something else. He says he doesn't want any more of this medicine—I don't blame him. But of course we must continue....God please give me the strength to keep encouraging Matt. I marvel at Matt's complete trust and cooperation—please, God, don't let him down.

Day by day, as Matt's leukemic cells were being destroyed, the side-effects worsened. Most transplant patients during this time develop mucositis. These are painful sores that develop throughout the mouth and esophagus, making it almost impossible to swallow, eat, or drink. Our friend and fellow transplant patient, eight-year-old Keith, developed mucositis, and we saw how much he suffered.

Matt never developed mucositis—I don't know why. Instead, his gastro-intestinal system was severely affected. Matt's symptoms were ongoing nausea and vomiting and diarrhea. The "red bucket" was his constant companion, as we never knew when he would throw up. He also developed the "moon facies" (the chubby cheeks from the high doses of Prednisone, one of the anti-leukemic drugs). Because he was self-conscious of his appearance, with a bald head, extremely enlarged cheeks, the droopy smile, Matt did not want his picture taken at all. Yet, he quietly endured his treatments, his scans to check the status of his cancer, and the numerous doctors' visits, nurse interventions, and required exercise regime.

11/17/1986—8:35 A.M.—Maureen
The night went better—Matt fell asleep about 9 P.M. M and had his Ara-C at midnight. He only threw up twice. He said, "I think I'm doing better, Mom." He's such a courageous little boy and just takes all these new things a step at a time.

The whole situation tends to make me want to pull in—gather our family together and shut out the whole rest of the world—yet, when people call or come by it's so helpful and we know they care and are so helped by their prayers and practical help. But we do get tired and worn out. It's a fine line and we haven't found the best answer yet. But we wouldn't trade the support of friends and family for anything.

Exercise regime? Yes, that's correct. Exercise regime! Matt's nurse, Theresa, placed a chart on the wall to keep track of Matt's plan for each day. He was to walk around the hall every day. Sometimes this meant pushing his sister Aimee in the wheelchair. I had a feeling this was her idea, but seeing her big smile as her brother pushed her around the unit was a blessing to me.

Life was brightened by the love and care of so many. My cousin Avis sent Matt a funny card every day and we looked forward to them and I loved seeing Matt laugh! Visitors were limited, but we could have short visits from friends. The girls were always allowed. They wore masks and washed their hands while in Matt's room. Matt wore the mask when he was in the hallway. Rich and I also were required to wear masks in Matt's room. I will always remember trying to sleep with the mask on. It was so uncomfortable and irritating. I had to remind myself this was nothing in comparison to what our Matt was going through.

As the treatments continued, Matt experienced additional symptoms. One of the drugs caused severe light sensitivity. He needed to wear sunglasses at all times. He remarked that his eyes hurt. Every part of Matt's body seemed to be affected—except still no mucositis. We were so thankful.

We saw the healthcare team work extremely hard to get the patients eating as much of a normal diet as possible. For the patients with mucositis, this was almost impossible. Also, medicines often change how food tastes, so many patients lose their appetite or refuse to eat. Each patient does receive nourishment through their Hickman line during their time in the hospital. Eating is an option, not required.

The patients could order whatever they wanted. The 10SW unit had its own chef who worked hard to make what the kids desired. In Matt's case, nothing tasted good, and he would just throw up whatever he took in. One day the chef came to talk with Matt and asked him if there was anything that sounded good. Matt, in his always quiet manner, said a Taco Time burrito sounded good. That wonderful man rushed out of the hospital and drove to the nearest Taco Time and brought Matt his burrito! I think we were all shocked when he came in with that gift! That is only one demonstration of how passionately the entire staff cared for Matt and our family. I am eternally grateful for the gift of that man to our son—to offer him some positive in a sea of struggles. Matt did eat the burrito!

11/20/1986—Maureen

Matt and Rich are down at the Tumor Institute for his last bit of cranial radiation—thank you, Lord!!

Rich said he had a better night, but now has some diarrhea—please strengthen Matt as he goes through his treatments.

11/22/1986—9 A.M.—Rich

Matt's eyes are better and he's watching cartoons with his Disneyland sunglasses on. More grapefruit for breakfast—this time with Pepsi. Pineapple juice helped flush the Bactrim (antibiotic) down. Matt received his last dose of Ara-C yesterday and had a good day. I worked until 12:30 P.M. and then went home. Sheryl (our neighbor) brought Aimee, and Carol (our friend) brought Kristy home after I got home. Kristy has a hard-hitting cold. Please, Lord, help her get over it before transplant. This adds a complication—Matt doesn't need a cold virus.

As we got nearer and nearer to Day 0, the day of the transplant, our hopes grew. The thought of being on the healing side and finished with the devastating effects of chemotherapy and radiation on Matt's body filled us with eager anticipation. The transplant was tentatively set for November 26, appropriately the day before Thanksgiving.

Our dear friends Dwayne and Lorelle brought Kristy to the hospital the night before transplant to get her admitted as the donor. Their daughter, Elizabeth, was four-year-old Kristy's best friend. She was on the third floor, Pediatrics. Matt was on the tenth floor. It was so difficult to have two of our children in the hospital at the same time, and I was so torn as to what room I needed to be in. I wished I could be in both places at the same time. I'll never forget walking into a room filled with squeals and giggles, as I found that Elizabeth and Kristy had raised the hospital beds to the highest level and were jumping up and down on the beds!! All I could think was, please don't let Kristy break a bone or do anything to delay the transplant tomorrow! There was some serious talking done to two little girls about proper hospital activities.

I think both Rich and I were a bundle of emotions that night—anxiety, excitement, fear, anticipation. Neither one of us slept much that night. We prayed and prayed for God's peace and protection for Matt and Kristy and that the procedure would be a success. Tomorrow was Day 0!

Chapter 10

Day 0! Transplant Day!!

"Peace I leave with you; My peace I give to you; not as world gives do I give to you. Do not let your heart be troubled, nor let it be fearful." John 14:27 (ESV)

November 26th—Matt gets his transplant. All the waiting and praying and enduring so many treatments and procedures have come down to today.

Rich and I accompanied Kristy to the surgical suite, where the physicians would harvest her bone marrow for her brother. Kristy always viewed each new experience with excitement and enthusiasm. This was no exception. The anesthesiologist met us in the hallway to explain the procedure and administer the anesthesia. As we waited with him for the anesthesia to take effect, Kristy chatted on enthusiastically! After a few minutes passed and she was still not asleep, the anesthesiologist gave her another dose of medicine. It took three doses before Kristy finally fell asleep.

God's hand was visibly present on her during this time. Her positive attitude was a blessing to her dad and me. It gave us such a sense of peace that she didn't seem scared or anxious. I know she was also excited about the presents that would await her after the procedure.

The physicians came out to see us after the procedure. They told us that Kristy was a trooper during the surgery. She was also helpful and held the mask over her face for the anesthesiologist. We thought for sure she would be a doctor!! For the donor, the procedure includes 250-300 needle punches over the sacrum to remove the bone marrow. It is an extensive process and we realized what a sacrifice it was for Kristy to go through this experience. We got the okay to see her. A very pale but healthy little four-year-old was in the recovery room. I was so thankful to see her and that she had come through the procedure well. Rich went up to let Matt know his little sister was okay, and I stayed with our Kristy.

As a rule, I never told the healthcare professionals that I was a nurse—my role was a mom and I didn't want them to expect more of me because I was a nurse. I wasn't a transplant nurse by any means. That's why I was so surprised to be left alone in the recovery room with Kristy. There were no other nurses present. Who would take her vital signs? Who would make sure she recovered okay? No one appeared, so I faithfully took Kristy's vital signs, made sure she was stabilized, and accompanied her to her room, a little bit shaken, but grateful.

When we got to Kristy's hospital room, Kristy awakened and the first words out of her mouth were "Where are my presents?" She'd seen Matt's room and knew something special was about to happen. My mom was waiting there with Aunt Maudie, a stuffed kitten for her granddaughter. My mom gave her the kitten and she just smiled and hugged it. Kristy was a very pale gray color, but herself. My heart was so full and I'll be forever grateful for the gift Kristy gave to her brother.

Rich stayed in Kristy's room to be with her as she recovered. I went up to join Matt to let him know Kristy was doing well. There was an air of expectation in the room that was unspoken between Matt and me. We didn't need to say anything. I believe that he knew the importance of this moment. He was a boy of few words but great understanding.

The nurses came in to hang Kristy's bone marrow. My heart was pounding, as I saw them connect this lifesaving fluid into our little boy. All our hopes rested on this long-anticipated moment. The weeks of treatments and painful procedures had all led to this. Kristy's bone marrow began its slow infusion and Matt and I continued our activities—Matt sorting baseball cards and me reading. I was so surprised that there was so little fanfare for this moment by the staff. I guess in my perfect world, there would be a bold pronouncement that "here it is," and we would all stand around and celebrate its arrival. Instead, it was very matter-of-fact. It looked like Matt was receiving a regular blood transfusion, although still serious, not the same impact of receiving new bone marrow and hope for a cure.

Rich later brought Kristy up to Matt's room so that she could see her bone marrow infusing into her brother's body. We just held our little girl and hugged her. I don't think she could fully grasp the incredible gift that she was providing for her brother.

Matt was very matter-of-fact. As he watched the bone marrow infusing, he asked, "Does this mean I have girl's blood?" Always a boy!

Now began the waiting process....

11/26/1986—Maureen
Well, Lord, today is the day. Matt's new marrow from Kristy is infusing.... Praise God!! And Kristy's recuperating!! Thank you, Lord!! Matt's temperature is still up about 103 so they have him on a cooling blanket. Oh, Lord, we pray for healing and safety as we wait for the new marrow to grow in. Kristy just came up to see Matt—a little pale, but doing great. She's loving all the attention and presents—Rich got some pictures of the two of them together that will surely be treasures. We are so surrounded by prayer and love and caring. It's so good to have Aimee here—our whole family is at least together.

Now we are a day 0 and even though there are some expected rough days ahead of us, we are also on the way to some healing. Now we can count in positive numbers and now we can look for healing signs.

Chapter 11

Living One Day at a Time

For I the Lord your God
Hold your right hand;
It is I who say to you, "Fear not,
I am the one who helps you." Isaiah 41:13

The day after transplant was indeed a day of Thanksgiving, as well as Thanksgiving Day! Honestly, we had not even thought of Thanksgiving this year. Our focus had been on Matt's transplant. Our wonderful neighbors, Steve and Laurie, asked if they could bring Thanksgiving dinner to us. Of course, how could we not forget to celebrate this holiday? Aimee and Kristy needed some familiar events in their lives, and we had so much to be thankful for this year.

On 10SW, the unit has a family room, where family members and visitors can eat, watch TV, or just relax and have a space away from their patient's room. There was a refrigerator in the room, where all the families kept food carefully labeled with the patient's name. Tables for families and friends to eat together were placed throughout the room.

Our neighbors brought the entire traditional meal, from cranberries and turkey to pumpkin pie. The table was decorated beautifully. After setting the table, they wisely left so we could enjoy the meal with our girls. Again, a little piece of normalcy for our daughters in a crazy world. I will always treasure that gift to our family.

As we continued the positive days, counting each one with hope for healing, a new routine was established. Rich and I continued to take turns spending the night with Matt, and trying to preserve some sense of normalcy for our girls with school, friends, and times with their brother.

After donating the marrow, most adult patients have difficulty walking for several days related to the pain from the multiple punctures of the sacrum. Not so much, Kristy. The day after donation, Kristy was up and riding a Big Wheels bike through the halls of the third floor. For me, this was another of God's miracles. To see her up and around and not experiencing pain was amazing! She loved all the attention, presents, and being her positive self, she greeted the day with excitement! Kristy was discharged that same day, so she was able to be with Matt in his room and the rest of the family.

Each morning we would wait for the results of Matt's blood draws. A report with the results of would be given to us each day. After the blood cells are decreased to zero before transplant, the critical item to watch is for the growth of new blood cells. Typically, the numbers increase daily as they start to appear, multiplying with each report. That would be the sign that the new bone marrow was growing healthy cells. Day after day, we would receive the report on Matt's numbers; very few cells appeared. It seemed like an eternity to Rich and me, as we eagerly sought to see this multiplication of blood cells. We were told to expect 100s and 1000s of new cells each morning. Matt's numbers were 1 or 2 new blood cells. The physicians told us Matt's response was sluggish. His cell growth was very, very slow. We continued to hold on to hope. The other concern was Graft versus Host Disease (GVHD), which occurs when the recipient's body fights against the new cells as not recognizable or foreign. Matt was on medications to prevent the rejection of the new blood cells, and we constantly looked for signs that the transplanted cells were accepted.

11/30/1986 — Rich

Day 4 coming up. No signs of GVHD and no bothersome mouth sores. Matt has been feeling fine except for the once a day fevers and constant diarrhea. Matt's eye-hand coordination is as good as ever—he can routinely beat me in the various Atari games. We just finished 3 laps (around the unit) and the doctors are making rounds. Ellyn watched Matt and let Maureen and me go to Red Robin for dinner. Bah (Maureen's mother) brought Kristy back to our house after a night with her and Uncle Charles and Aunt Aileen. Aimee spent the last two nights at the Ibachs (family friends). Today is Sunday and Maureen will take the girls to church.

Fred Hutchinson Cancer Research Center was an amazing place. Not only did they provide cutting-edge treatment for cancer patients, they cared for the whole family. One of the resources they provided was the Hutch School. It was a school for siblings or children of transplant patients who were from out of town and provided a way to continue their education until they were home again. They also provided activities for the children. Aimee and Kristy loved the crafts and activities that served to distract them from their brother's struggles.

We had wonderful visitors from time to time. One night as we neared the holidays, a hammered dulcimer and flute duet played outside each patient's door. Seattle Seahawks came to visit the kids—Matt got to meet our quarterback, Dave Kreig.

However, Matt was an avid baseball fan. He had played Little League passionately before he got sick, and his dad was his coach. He loved the Seattle Mariners team and longed to "meet a Mariner." In fact, in the initial Make-A-Wish visit, that was one of his wishes. At night, when we would pore over and organize and reorganize his 200+ baseball cards, he would share about his favorite players. Alvin Davis, the Mariner's first baseman, was his favorite. So, he was a little disappointed when a Mariner was scheduled to come visit him but it wasn't Alvin Davis. It was Mark Langston, the pitcher. Trying to be diplomatic and ease his disappointment, I pulled out his statistics book and we read about Mark. Matt was thrilled to learn that he was voted Rookie of the Year and was an outstanding player! So, his attitude changed completely! He was excited to meet him.

The afternoon came for Mark's visit. His agent waited in the hallway with Mark's six-month-old baby in his arms. Mark came into a very sick little boy's room and spent 45 minutes talking just to him. Not to me, the mother, but to Matt. I was so thankful and always will be to him. He quickly became Matt's new favorite

Mariner! Matt sheepishly told Mark that Alvin Davis was initially his first choice, and Mark laughed and said, "That's okay, he's my roommate and my good friend."

There were so many special times during those fifty days at the Hutch. The staff, the volunteers, the physicians, the other patients. Each blessed our family's life in many ways.

12/1/1986—Maureen

We made it to December! Thank you Lord! Matt is listless and restless—nothing to do. Last night at 11:15 PM he wanted to take a walk-so we did 3 laps. What a special little boy! He is going through so much. Last night his prayer was, "Lord, help me get through all this."

Aimee and Kristy seem to be doing well—I'm amazed at them, too! Kristy flew through the bone marrow harvest surgery with almost no pain—was never afraid or scared—thank you, Lord! The doctors told us she's destined for a career in medicine maybe...Aimee wanted so much to go to the Hutch school, but Rich is right—so, she's back in school and that may do her as much good, too.

12/4/1986—Maureen

Some days it's so hard to write in the journal, because I don't feel like it—but, I realize this is important and I will be glad I did take the time and energy to write. Matt is on day 8—praise the Lord—he's still having diarrhea—fevers are less—but his blood pressure is still up and down. His new complaint is tummy pain—the morphine they began Tuesday really helps and doesn't really make him sleepy. Matt felt better last night—we watched a special program on how they made the Superman movie and then he wanted to play video games, so we did—that lasted until 10:40 PM. With MUCH prompting, he did his laps, complaining all the way, and he also did two miles on his exercise bike.

12/11/1986—Maureen

Good morning, Lord. Decided it was a good time to write my prayer this AM as I'm having difficulty praying without interruptions, etc. First, I want to thank you and praise you for providing spicules (bone marrow particles) in Matt's marrow. I know statistics don't matter to You—that You are above all of that—but I still get scared. I ask You to increase my faith and trust.

I pray for Aimee and Kristy that you would hold them close these days—give them understanding and not bitterness. Keep them protected at school and home and with friends. They are such special little girls and I thank you for them. Help Aimee not be too hard on herself and help Kristy to continue to be loving.

Hold Matt extra close—he is a special little boy. Give him strength and peace and trust...help him to share his feelings and his concerns with us so that we can encourage and support him. Please heal him, Lord.

Day by day, the blood counts began to- come in, and we saw growth from Kristy's bone marrow. We were overjoyed! Christmas was approaching and once again, we were surrounded by the love and care of friends and family. Our Christmas presents were purchased and wrapped by them, our girls were taken shopping, and an anonymous financial gift was brought to us from one of our pastors. We were overwhelmed!

Rich and I had much different attitudes that Christmas season from other years, since beginning the journey with Matt's cancer. I like to call it stripped down to the bare basics. The priorities shifted: It was no longer the gifts and cards, but time. Time spent together as a family—time that we knew was not guaranteed. We were cautiously optimistic that the bone marrow transplant would be successful and Matt would be healed. Yet, as we looked around our floor, we saw the statistics in real-life examples. We had already lost fellow patients Michael, Todd, and baby Jessica. We were thankful that Keith was doing well, because he was Matt's buddy on the floor.

We were also anxious to take Matt home for Christmas Day. The physicians told us it could be a possibility, depending on his blood counts. They were still low, but Rich and I were so hopeful to bring Matt home to celebrate as a family in our home.

Christmas morning, we awoke with that hope in the forefront of our minds. I was already picturing our whole family at home around the Christmas tree opening presents. That would be a little slice of normal. As I waited for his daily counts to come in, Matt and I talked about what he wanted for Christmas—a BMX bike! I had to swallow hard, knowing that he had so few platelets, that if he fell, he risked bleeding without the ability to clot his blood. Platelets are the components of our blood that are responsible for clotting the blood and preventing hemorrhages. The normal range is 150,000-450,000 platelets. Matt's platelet count had been running around 5000-6000. I had to remember that he still had the normal desires of a typical almost eight-year-old boy. He needed a bike. Rich and I had purchased a BMX bike weeks earlier, in the hopes that he would be able to ride it at some time in the future. Little did we know that Christmas would be the time!

We finally got the news—the blood counts were back up and he could go home!! Matt donned his mask and we headed for home.

I treasured every moment that Christmas. It was a sunny, clear day—unusual for Seattle. After we opened our presents, Rich brought the bike for Matt to open. He was so excited and wanted to ride it immediately! Our whole family headed outside to see Matt try out his new bike. I can still see his huge grin as he rode around and around the island in front of our house. I prayed and prayed that he wouldn't fall and my prayers were answered.

It was a glorious day, and I didn't want to see it come to an end. Once more we made the trip back to the hospital. The rest of the week was routine, meaning hospital tests, results from those tests, rounding by the physicians, and hoping and praying that Kristy's bone marrow was growing and thriving inside of Matt. Friends visited with love and encouragement, family took care of our girls and our home, and once again, we were supplied with meals. Rich's brother, Mike, and our pastor, Jim Groenink, each spent one night at the hospital so that Rich and I could go home together. We had not realized how long it had been that we went home together. What a gift that was!

12/27/1986—Maureen
Here we are on day 31—a day I thought we'd be home and out of the hospital—but, things don't always go according to my hopes and dreams and plans. Matt's doing very well—we're just waiting for some counts to come in—it's in Your hands, Lord, and I trust in You knowing Matt is in Your hands. But I'm impatient, Lord—You know that about me—thank You for allowing us to go home on Christmas day. That was the best gift of all. Seeing Matt ride his bike and so excited.

Dear Lord, please let Matt go home soon—having had a taste of it—I'm all the more eager and I trust your perfect timing, Lord, and praise You for healing Matt.

The days rolled from one to another, and we lived moment by moment, awaiting lab results each morning, and seeing Matt grow stronger each day. God continued to provide energy, strength, and peace to me, through the gifts of friends, scripture verses that drew me close to Him. It became more and more apparent to me that He was the only One I could depend on, and I was completely dependent on Him.

Chapter 12
The Community of 10SW

Let your speech always be with grace, as though
seasoned with salt, so that you will know how you
should respond to each person. Col. 4:6

Twenty-four patients and their families made up the community of
10SW. Patients ranged in age from six months to adult. They were
from all over the world, and we became attached to many of them
and their families.

The floor was set up in a connected square arrangement with the
treatment stations, nurses' station, utility rooms, medicine rooms,
and conference rooms in the center. At one end of the hall was the
Intensive Care Unit, from which not one patient came out alive during
our time there. Next to that was the family room, where the families
of the ICU patients could gather. At the opposite end of the unit was
a large family room and kitchen. It was a great place to meet visitors,
as they weren't allowed in Matt's room because of his suppressed
immune system, unless they wore masks and had our permission.

Families all drew together through suffering and adversity. The
staff warned us not to get to know the other patients, but how could
you not? We were blessed by them and hopefully blessed them in
return. We knew that we were all facing our patient's poor
prognoses, because remember, the Hutch only took the hard cases
that no one else wanted.

The Murphys: What a gift from God to us. We met them early in our stay and their son Keith and Matt became fast friends. They were from Boise, Idaho. Keith had Acute Lymphocytic Leukemia (ALL) and had relapsed. He had only a 10% chance of survival because of the relapse and he had lost more than 20% of his body weight. He was a year older than Matt at eight years of age. John and Loretta had three other children; eleven-year-old Jason, six-year-old Heather, and two-year-old Derek. Keith had asked Make-A-Wish for a horse and a driving car, and Matt was impressed that Keith had received them. He drove the car around the halls all the time. They were Christians also, and we found our shared faith a source of strength. Keith is alive today, married, and living in Idaho. He was the only survivor from that group of twenty-four patients.

Michael Moore: Aged 18, he was in the room next to us. We met him in the hall wearing a Santa Claus hat and a big smile. We were touched by his love of life and giving heart. Michael and his family were from Louisiana. He was one of the patients that went to the ICU and didn't return.

Todd and Susan: Todd was a young man in his twenties, newly married to Susan and from Boston. They were two doors down from us. Todd had been placed in a Laminar Air Flow Room, so we could only talk to him through the plastic curtain. Susan amazed us in her love and strength through Todd's illness. He was a computer whiz and wrote gaming programs for computers—something he continued to do throughout his transplant. We befriended Susan, as they were from the East Coast and had no family here. When Todd was transferred to the ICU, we grieved for them both. Susan was distraught. Rich went down to see her in the ICU family room and asked her over and over if there was anything he could do for her. After turning down his many attempts, Susan finally agreed that she'd like a glass of milk. Rich literally ran down the hall as fast as he could and carried that milk to Susan like it was a gift of gold.

Suddenly, he realized how wonderful it felt to help her, even in a very small way. Here we had been turning down offer after offer of help, saying no, we were fine. Rich realized and shared with me that we were robbing our friends and family of that amazing gift of being able to do something to help to lessen someone's pain. It was a turning point in our journey and we began to let people in to help. Sadly, Todd didn't return from the ICU. We kept in touch with Susan for a long time, and she even visited us in Seattle years later. We will always hold her close in our hearts.

Crystal: I think she was about four years old. She had a huge family, lots of brothers and sisters, and a wonderful mom and dad. She had a lot of joy and love surrounding her. When Crystal went to the ICU, we were so worried and prayed she would survive. She didn't, but we were able to attend her memorial service. It was attended by several hundred people. It was a moving tribute to her and her family.

Baby Jessica: She was about six months old and had ALL. Her family was wonderful—we loved her mom so much. Matt and I were walking around the halls—fulfilling the required exercise regime—and we saw baby Jessica in the ICU, hooked up to tubes and IVs. Matt looked in the room and looked at me and said, "Mom, please don't ever let me go to the ICU." Jessica never came out.

I could go on and on—we cried and laughed with the families. Yes, laughed, as there was still life to live, despite daily crises with our patients. Matt and Keith, with their masks and bald heads, would play Nerf baseball in the elevator lobby. They would ride up and down in the elevators. They were typical little boys dealing with extraordinary life circumstances.

Chapter 13

New Year's Eve, 1986

"He gives strength to the weary
And to him who lacks might He increases power.
Though youths grow weary and tired,
And vigorous young men stumble badly,
Yet those who wait for the Lord
Will gain new strength;
The will mount up with wings like eagles,
They will run and not get tired,
They will walk and not become weary."
Isaiah: 40:29-31

The end of the year was approaching, and it was New Year's Eve day. My dear friend Kris Bemis came by to offer me a respite from the hospital room. She offered to stay with Matt so that I could take a walk around the hospital. Wistfully, I left Matt and started out with mixed feelings. Something in my heart told me I shouldn't leave. God's hand once again. As I started walking over the skybridge, I had the urge to return immediately. Kris was kneeling beside Matt's bedside and reading him a story. I was so thankful to and appreciative of her heart to love our son in real and tangible ways. At the same time, I knew my place was with Matt and it didn't feel right to leave him then. Lovingly, Kris said she understood.

New Year's Eve arrived, and we had planned a big party in the family room with all of Matt's friends and family. It was a tradition, as Matt's birthday was January 1st. As we prepared for the party, the physicians called us into the conference room. Remembering that Matt always asked for the physicians to give us any news in his room, we went into the conference room full of trepidation. Our experience led us to expect bad news.

Rich and I entered the conference room and there were all Matt's physicians, social workers, and others that I didn't know assembled around the table. There must have been 20 people there. We took our seats and prepared for the worst. One of the doctors began to speak. The news wasn't good. Matt's most recent bone marrow aspiration had shown leukemic cells. The bone marrow transplant had failed. They apologized for the results and announced that treatment would stop, including the anti-rejection drugs.

I was numb. I didn't know what to say. Somehow, I squeaked out, "How long does he have to live?" I had to know. The doctors gently told me that they could never be sure, but they figured about two weeks. For some reason, I asked, "How will he die?" Where that question came from, I'll never know. I think Rich and I both needed to know, but neither of us wanted to ask the question. We were told that, usually, because of a weakened immune system, pneumonia would probably be the cause.

As I sat there, I felt that all hope was gone. One thing that cancer patients and their families cling to is hope. Cancer is such an unpredictable disease, one cannot always predict how the body will respond. So, hope is always present, until the very last moment. I wondered if this was that moment. The physicians expressed their sorrow and care and we got up to leave. Jennifer, one of the social workers, came up to me and pressed a piece of paper in my hand. On it was printed: "The Northwest Center for Attitudinal Healing." I was so thankful to her—she had not given up hope! So, I was not going to give up either. If one person thought Matt could survive, I could have hope.

The sensitive nurses led Rich and me to a quiet office and shut the door. Rich and I looked at each other and began to cry. We must have stood there holding each other and crying for several minutes, when Rich asked, "How do we tell Matt?" How could we tell our son? How could we tell him that all the painful, horrible procedures didn't kill the cancer? How could we tell him that all the sacrifices he made were in vain?

I'm so thankful to my husband, that he could think clearly and rationally at that time. I don't know how parents do this by themselves. Rich was my rock. He would tell Matt the best that he could. Quickly, we began to call all the people coming to Matt's party that night and cancelled. Then we headed to Matt's room to give him the news.

I believe that Matt already knew—mostly because of our trip to the conference room. Rich sat down next to him on his bed and told him that his cancer had come back. Matt took a deep breath, was silent for a few seconds, and then asked, "Does this mean I'm going to die?" Rich now took a deep breath, and gently told him, "Matt, we are all going to die, but we are going to pray that God will heal you and you will beat this cancer."

Then Matt said the words that only an almost eight-year-old boy would say: "Can I still have my party?" Rich and I both smiled at each other and said together, "Yes! Absolutely!"

Quickly we grabbed the phone and called everyone back and told them the party was still on. It took a little bit of explaining, but everyone was supportive and eager to have the best party ever! They provided a heavenly distraction for what lay ahead for Matt and our family. We were so thankful.

Chapter 14
The New Year Begins

"Trust in the Lord with all your heart, and do not
lean on your own understanding
In all your way acknowledge him, and he will make
straight your paths." Proverbs 3:5-6 (ESV)

Once a patient has relapsed after the transplant, they are quickly "kicked out" of the system. So, we were sent home the next morning. It was Matt's eighth birthday. We had invited all his friends, because we wanted to make it a special celebration. We realized it could be his last birthday. Matt was only supposed to be around two or three people at a time, because of his compromised immune system. As we had broken all the other rules so far, we had forty-plus people to our home. I'll never forget the sight of Matt vacuuming the living room with his mask on, to make sure everything was perfect for his party. I always lined up the "vacuum lines" on the carpet and he was sure to do that, too.

What a glorious celebration! People were so wonderful to Matt—no sadness, no tears, just a celebration of his life and a typical eight-year-old birthday party! Well, maybe not so typical, since Matt had to remove his mask to blow out the candles.

Where do we go from here? That was the question I kept asking myself. I had learned to trust God for every moment, one moment at a time. I couldn't see far enough to trust minutes or hours or days.

Just moments. God was so faithful—for me, a woman with so many fears and doubts, to be able to survive was truly a miracle. God's gift of His grace was so evident to me as we moved closer and closer to the two-week life-expectancy prediction the doctors had made.

The month went by slowly. We were transferred back to Children's Hospital for follow-up.

1/21/1987—Maureen
Good Morning, Lord.

I sure fell off my journal entries—when we got word of Matt's relapse—I just couldn't write anymore. I couldn't pray or think—it was like being paralyzed—-but I know You are holding me in all of this—holding us all through these difficult times and I thank You and praise You for that.

Please protect Aimee, Matt, and Kristy and keep them safe—healthy—help me be sensitive to their needs and let them know I love them.

1/23/1987 – Maureen
What can I say but thank you, Lord! I praise You and give You all the glory and love and honor. You indeed do mighty things. The song is saying God is so good—You are, Lord. I love You!

Matthew is doing so well, Lord, and it's all because of the miracle You are doing in him—You are so real to us and so near because of what we've gone through with Matt's leukemia—I can praise You in this circumstance because I see us all drawing closer to You and because of Rich's giant leap in faith. Thank you, Jesus. I never thought I could say that—but because of You all things do work together for good for those who love You.

Rich wanted to pack a lifetime into those two weeks. Matt wanted to go camping. So, we went camping! A dear couple in our church loaned us their RV and we loaded up the kids and the dog and all of Matt's medicines and IVs and headed out. January is not a typical camping month in Seattle, but we made it work. Board games around the RV's kitchen table, the kids sleeping on the top bunk of the RV. One of my favorite memories was the next morning when the park ranger came into our RV to collect the camping fees, and saw the syringes, needles, and IV tubing spread all over the table. He raised an eyebrow, but didn't say a word. I wonder what he was thinking we were doing there, in an isolated campground with all the paraphernalia.

We spent time with Keith and his family. Keith had been readmitted to the hospital, fighting an infection, so we went to visit him. When he was discharged, we all went to the movies together, played in the park, and did normal kid things. Both families took the ferry to Victoria, BC, and had a great time shopping and exploring that quaint city. We are forever thankful to the Murphys for the blessing they were to us.

A strange thing was occurring as the month went on. Matt was getting better, not worse. His GVHD was rampant—constant itching and his skin was peeling. The doctors had taken Matt off all the medicines, including his anti-rejection medicine, so that allowed the GVHD to thrive.

We had an appointment at Children's Hospital, just before my birthday, January 25. All that I could think was that the only birthday gift I wanted was for Matt to be healed. As we met with Dr. Barbra Clark, the head of the oncology clinic, she asked if Matt and I would come with her to the lab and look in the microscope. She showed Matt a slide of his bone marrow tissue. She asked him what he saw. "Nothing" was his reply. Then she showed Matt a slide of a leukemic bone marrow, and asked him the same question again. It was full of leukemic cancer cells.

At that moment, I received my best birthday present—there was no sign of cancer in Matt's bone marrow!! He was healed!! It took a moment for that to sink in. Dr. Clark was overjoyed and then we were, too! God had answered my prayers!

As we drove home from the hospital appointment, I asked Matt what he wanted to do with his life now that God had healed him. "I want to be a pastor so that I can help people," he said, "but I also want to be a racecar driver, so that I can be rich." Spoken like a typical eight-year-old little boy!

My heart overflowed with gratitude for God's grace and the gift of life for our son. It seemed almost too good to be true, after the roller-coaster of emotions and events that we had experienced over the last few months. I knew God was sovereign, that He was in control. I knew He could heal Matt. Yet, comprehending that He truly had healed him against all odds was overwhelming. My heart felt like it would burst, and I couldn't wait to tell Rich and the girls the miraculous news! God is so good! His hand continued to be on Matt and our whole family, and I believed He desired for me to trust Him and depend on Him alone.

One of our promises to Matt during transplant was that if he went along with all the treatments, kept up with his schoolwork, and exercised, he could play Little League in the spring. We were hoping upon hope that he would live that long. The very next day, we went and signed Matt up for Little League.

2/10/1987—Maureen

Good Morning Father. My heart and whole being are overflowing with love and praise for You. I am so humbled and filled with awe. Thank you, Lord.

First on January 28, You gave us the glorious news that Matt's bone marrow aspiration was normal! Praise You!! And now, we have the glorious news that his chromosomes—cytogenetics—are Kristy's and normal! How we thank you and praise You!! I am overwhelmed1 And because of Your miracles so many people are blessed and their faith is increased.

Little did we know that God had healed Matt for a baseball season.

Chapter 15

The Quiet before the Storm

"He has said to me; my grace is sufficient for you..."
2 Cor. 12:9

Long-term follow-up!! I was overjoyed that we were sent back to Fred Hutchinson! Since Matt's bone marrow showed no more signs of leukemia, he was declared healed and we were transferred to the Bone Marrow Transplant's Long-Term Follow-up clinic. Our first appointment was a celebration. Matt's Hickman line was removed—a huge step in getting better.

We met with our favorite Australian doctor, Dr. Cyrus Hill, for a summary of care. Rich asked him what had cured Matt. We knew that God had worked a miracle. Dr. Hill smiled and said, after some thought, "I don't know, but if I did, we'd offer it to everyone." The impact of Matt's healing was just beginning to sink in for our family. We made regular trips to Fred Hutch for long-term follow-up to aid in the statistic gathering for transplant. It still was an experimental program.

A few weeks later, we got together with Keith and his family, to celebrate our one hundred days of survival after treatment! What a celebration it was! Two little boys with a shadow of hair appearing on their bald heads, and with huge grins on their faces, as they blew out the candles on the 100-day cake!

Journal Entry: 3/1/1987—Maureen

Here we are at day 109 and still praising God for Matt's miracle. I hope we never stop. Matt has done so well—and we are still incredulous at his courage and perception. He can't decide if he wants to be a "Big Foot" driver or a scientist or both. But he does want to get a corvette!

People are so good to us. We had a wonderful sermon today by Joe Aldrich, the author of Lifestyle Evangelism. He spoke about loving people first and then leading them to the Lord. It seems so practical and I am so excited because of the testimony God has given us to share—Matt's miracle. I only pray I will let God use me to share the Lord with others.

Little League season was scheduled to start, with Rich returning to his role of coaching these little boys. As we did frequently, I met my mom with the kids for lunch. As we sat in the restaurant, my mom said she had noticed a lump on the side of Matt's neck. Panic hit me...why had I not noticed it? Matt was focused on his Little League season, and I guess I must have been, too.

3/6/1987—Maureen

Anxieties and fear have set in again—I'm so disappointed in my reactions. Today at lunch, Mom pointed out some swelling on the left side of Matt's neck—she had noticed it last Thursday. I felt it—it's very hard—and I immediately panicked and thought tumor. So, I buried that all inside, went through the rest of the afternoon, and by about 4:15 or 4:30, my anxieties were so high, I had to do something.

So, I called Diane Heye at Fred Hutch—she said she wasn't sure—said it could be Burkitt's, but she didn't know—need to have Dr. Clark check it tomorrow. I called Children's and who should answer the phone, but Dr. Clark! Thank you, Lord! So, I asked her—she felt comfortable sharing it was a swollen lymph node—I pray with all my heart she's right. She told me not to worry—but I am—I'm a basket case right now, Lord! Oh, Lord, please help me to trust you—to keep my eyes upon You. You have healed Matt. Please don't let these fears consume me—please let me remember You are still in control.

Ruefully, I called and scheduled an appointment at Children's Hospital after speaking with the doctors at Fred Hutch. The recommended next step was a biopsy of the lump. As we left the hospital, after the biopsy, I found a note, one of many I would find, from my dear friend, Ellyn. "Our God Reigns!!" was all that it said, and I was reminded again that He is in control. We are not in this battle alone.

The results of the biopsy were what we feared...Burkitt's Lymphoma. My heart sunk. Once again, the dogged determination took over my mind and we set back into the routine of treatments mixed with hope that they would be successful. This time the plan was different—Matt's body could not handle the maximum doses of radiation and chemotherapy because he had maxed out during the transplant.

Matt's care was transferred back to Children's Hospital, where our journey had begun. Chemotherapy was ordered, and we once again began the trips back and forth across the lake to the clinic. We fell in love with the staff, and our doctor, Barbara Clark. She was like a grandmother to Matt and she provided us with so much hope and strength. Matt's chemotherapy consisted of three hours of IV infusion through his Hickman (number two placed) and I would sit and knit while Matt slept or watched videos. Every time, he got to choose something from the Red Box, and usually it was a He-Man figure.

The tumor began to shrink, but because Burkitt's is so virulent, the doctors recommended radiation at the same time. This was to be done in the basement of the University of Washington Hospital, where a large radiation clinic was located. As we came to our first treatment, we saw many patients in the waiting room of various ages and with varying amounts of hair. Once again, we were in the world of cancer treatment. Matt was measured for the radiation treatment, with permanent markers all over his head and neck to make sure the radiation was aimed at the right location. Our technicians were compassionate, funny, and wonderful to Matt. We grew to love them, also. Matt was so well cared for and all our doctors, nurses, and technicians became like family.

Spring break came, and our wonderful daughters spent the week with Matt and me going to twice-a-day radiation treatments every day. I tried to make it fun, so in between treatments, we'd go to the video arcade and play games while we waited for the next treatment. Aimee and Kristy were amazing in their patience and support of their brother, and what our family was going through. They were only nine and four years of age, yet they were amazingly mature in their attitudes and understanding. I remember very little complaining or whining. We had a lot of fun during that spring break.

One day on the way to a radiation treatment, Matt and I were talking about the University of Washington stadium that was being enlarged and a new cantilevered side was being constructed. Because Rich was an engineer and built things, our family was used to noticing and commenting on construction projects. As we came out after treatment, we noticed the stadium was completely flattened. During our time in the clinic, the whole side of the stadium had collapsed because of a construction error! Matt and I could hardly wait to tell Rich what we'd seen.

As the weeks and months went by, Matt's condition worsened. The Burkitt's began to grow faster and faster, taking more of a toll on his body. The chemotherapy weakened his joints and made them extremely painful. The radiation caused his new hair to fall out. We continued to hope and plow on, but the anxiety and stress returned.

Matt continued in his Little League season. One could tell he was so happy to be playing his beloved baseball. The team of eight-year-old little boys was amazing. They supported and encouraged Matt as he struggled to play. He couldn't run very fast because of the chemotherapy. Still, the boys cheered him on whenever he got a hit. They overlooked his lack of hair and energy. They treated him like a normal little eight-year-old boy, when his life was anything but normal.

May came and we were getting ready for Kristy's 5th birthday party—a pony party at a little farm nearby. I noticed that the right side of Matt's face was drooping, and he told me he was seeing four of everything. Did this mean the cancer was in his brain? One thing I was learning with cancer was that any symptom, no matter how strange, was probably due to the cancer's spread. We had a great birthday party for Kristy on a beautiful day in May, and then headed to the hospital to have Matt evaluated.

Matt was a remarkable little boy. He had an inner sense and understanding that I came to respect. Whenever we headed out the door for an appointment, if Matt took his comforter, his puppet, Melford, and his pillow, it meant that we'd be admitted to the hospital. If he didn't, it meant it was just a clinic appointment.

This afternoon, Matt grabbed all three. Being a distracted mother at the time, I quickly said, "Matt, you don't need those—it's just a clinic appointment." Matt merely smiled at me and got in the car with his supplies in his arms. Sure enough, Matt was admitted that evening.

In the early days of transplant, the doctors told us that the time would come that we, as Matt's parents, would know more about Matt's treatment and illness than the doctors. That was almost frightening to us, as we didn't want that responsibility. We soon learned that they were right.

At the hospital, we learned that the cancer had spread to Matt's brain, so an Omaya reservoir was to be placed in Matt's head. This was a special insert that allowed the doctors to give chemotherapy directly into the brain. The procedure was brief, but required surgery once again. We met with the neurosurgeon, who very briefly explained the procedure. The surgery was to be done during the following week and Matt could be released three days later. The time and date would be determined by the surgeon's availability and schedule. Once again, I felt frustration at the delay, as we knew the viciousness of the Burkitt's cells rapid growth. Matt was once again admitted to Children's and again we waited.

During that time, Matt was still scheduled to receive his radiation treatments at the University of Washington, about a fifteen-minute drive away. On Friday, the day of surgery, the surgery was rescheduled many times during the morning. Rich felt he could wait no longer. Radiation was Matt's lifeline and the only true hope for a cure. We were his parents, and it didn't matter that Matt was an inpatient at Children's Hospital. Rich dutifully took Matt out of the hospital for his treatment at the nearby clinic as he knew he could be back in a short period of time.

Unfortunately, the surgery to place the Omaya was finally set and it was at the exact same time as Matt and Rich left. The surgical techs came to take Matt to surgery, and he was nowhere to be found. The doctors and nurses were frantic. We didn't realize that we were not to take Matt out of the hospital—all we knew was that Matt needed his radiation as scheduled, so we took responsibility to get it done. We had patiently waited for the surgery to be rescheduled, and were told it would be done as time allowed. Rich and I learned we should have told the nurses that Rich was taking Matt out of the hospital. Looking back, it makes sense, but we were focused on ensuring Matt received his radiation.

Rich returned with Matt after his radiation treatment to a very upset surgeon. He complained that we were upsetting his very important schedule. Rich was apologetic, but felt he did what was best for our son. Matt had his surgery, the Omaya reservoir was placed, and the surgery was successfully completed. We hoped we were done with any interaction with that surgeon.

One of the highlights of Matt's journey occurred next. The interns and residents came to see us on Saturday, full of excitement, and told us that the Mariners, Seattle's professional baseball team, were sponsoring a Little League Day, and had asked for a child to throw out the opening pitch against the Yankees. The doctors thought of Matt and asked if we'd consider letting him do that. The game was Sunday, the next day. Matt was overjoyed, and we knew this was a gift to him during all he was going through. We said yes without hesitation!!!

However, it meant taking Matt out of the hospital one day earlier than planned. The staff agreed it wouldn't be a problem, as Matt was doing fine. As we were getting ready to leave, the same now very angry neurosurgeon entered Matt's room. How dare we take Matt out early when his protocol stated he had to stay until Monday? We tried to explain that this was important to Matt, more important than his protocol, though we didn't say that part out loud. We were taking him home. In a very indignant voice, he said, "What do you want to do, take the stitches out yourselves, too?" I said calmly and firmly, "Yes, I can do that." He stomped out of the room, and we inwardly knew we'd won a small victory for our son.

Matt did throw out the opening pitch that Sunday in May. He and his dad practiced in the hallways outside the field. Matt could only see out of one eye and it was blurry, but he wanted to make sure he threw a good pitch. I was secretly a little disappointed that I couldn't go out on the field with him...I was the Mariners' fan! Inwardly, I knew, though, that Rich was the right choice...a dad and his son together. The catcher was Dave Valle, someone I'll be forever grateful to. As Matt walked out on the field with his dad, he looked so small in the giant Kingdome. Dave Valle moved forward, about halfway between home plate and the pitching mound——as Matt got ready to throw. He pitched a great ball and Dave instantly ran and gave Matt a big hug and the crowd cheered!

We knew that our time with Matt was precious, and that there were no guarantees that we'd have a week or a month more with him. We'd learned back in January that we needed to make the most of each day God gave us. The neurosurgeon meant well; he had his routines to follow. We realized that the doctors at the time of Matt's diagnosis were right, we did know better what Matt needed for treatment. Yes, he needed the treatments, but even more, he needed to have a chance to be a little boy. What eight-year-old boy would pass up a chance to pitch in a Major League Baseball game? Our priority was making each day special for him. After the pitch was thrown, Matt and his dad took their place in the stadium, Matt sitting on the edge of his seat with his mitt on his hand, waiting to catch that errant foul ball, should it come his way. It was about the quality of life.

Chapter 16
Trusting God for Each Day

"I am at rest in God alone;
My salvation comes from Him.
He alone is my rock and my salvation,
My stronghold; I will never be shaken."
Ps. 62:1-2 (HCSB)

The next few weeks were a blur of hospitalizations, appointments, new symptoms for Matt, and a slow understanding that Matt was losing his battle. We never gave up hope. Because of our experience with Matt's healing early on in his journey, we knew that God could do anything, and we trusted Him more than the doctors or medicines.

Matt was hospitalized one last time near the end of May 1987. The doctors determined that he had developed a Bell's Palsy and that was responsible for the paralysis of his face. They told us he didn't have long to live. We smiled and looked to God. Once again, Matt rallied, and the next morning he had improved. One of his doctors came in and was amazed. He didn't think Matt would make it through the night, and yet, here was his patient, sitting up in bed gobbling down a huge breakfast. Our trust had to be in God, or we'd have been buried in the number of bad prognoses.

The cancer ward I had initially dreaded became home to us once again. It now provided us with a sense of security. We knew the nurses and loved them. Rich and I loved Lynn, our nurse with the big smile and infectious laugh. I believed this was a gift from God to me, because I looked for her each day, as she gave us much joy. I was reminded once again of the nurse who had criticized me as a nursing student for smiling too much and they told me that wasn't appropriate around cancer patients. Are they kidding? I needed to see Lynn's smile and hear her laugh.

Matt was diagnosed with shingles, a very painful and contagious disease that forced our move to an isolation room on a different floor. I couldn't believe I didn't want to leave the cancer floor! But we understood, and made the transition to a new floor. It was a move away from our comfort zone and to a staff we didn't know.

Rich and I were back to trading nights at the hospital. As I crawled into bed at home, the phone rang about midnight. It was Rich. Matt had been brushing his teeth when he fell off his chair and his Hickman line came out! That was his lifeline, through which he got his medications, his fluids, and his nutrition. They would have to put it back in—number three—another surgery.

On the next day, Friday, June 5, Dr. Hickman inserted Matt's third Hickman line, as he had done each time before. It was my turn to spend the night with Matt. As he came back from surgery, all he wanted was a turkey dinner, complete with mashed potatoes and stuffing. Children's Hospital was incredible—whatever the kids want for food, they provide. Matt sat up in bed and ate the whole dinner—a big smile on his face!

It wasn't until months later, as I was reading Matt's medical records, that I learned his heart had stopped during the surgery and they had to resuscitate him. I'm thankful for every gift—including that I didn't know how close we came to losing him that night.

Chapter 17

One More Day

"The eternal God is your refuge, and underneath are the everlasting arms." Deuteronomy 33:27 (NIV)

The next day, early Saturday morning, we awoke to a beautiful, sunny day. Today was June 6, 1987, my dear friend Evie's birthday. Our friends Dwayne and Lorelle were helping with our girls. They lived near the hospital so they had offered to have Aimee and Kristy spend time with them.

Matt was not lacking in appetite, even after the huge turkey dinner the night before. He ordered and received a big breakfast, and ate the whole thing. He had come through surgery successfully and was cheerful and alert this morning. We were so hopeful. In the back of our minds, Rich and I both recalled that every time we received dire news about Matt's prognosis, he would rally. We thought that today would be the same. Matt's good appetite and happy demeanor encouraged us.

My mom came to visit us at the hospital. She was struggling seeing Matt so ill and was very upset. I wanted her to go away—to go home. She was making the situation worse. I couldn't take care of Matt and my mom at the same time. My ability to deal with stress or care for others was minimal. I knew she loved Matt and loved us, and I felt badly to be so angry with her.

The day seemed to be a typical day in the hospital with Matt. He did seem a little quieter and more reserved than usual. It was hard to tell, as he was normally quiet and reserved.

Dr. Clark came by that evening and explained to us that she had left orders for increasing doses of morphine to control Matt's pain—whatever he needed. The doctors had told us that Matt would not be in pain as the end neared; they would ensure that his pain could be controlled. At this point he was on low levels of morphine and seemed comfortable.

The doctors had explained to us that one of the side-effects of increasing doses of morphine was decreased respirations. As it controlled the pain, it also slowed the breathing, contributing to death, but a pain-free death. I remember having such mixed feelings, but I didn't want Matt to suffer. Rich and began to understand that the end might be near. We kept our hope and trust in God, remembering that He was still in control. His hand was on our son.

Matt's baseball team, the White Sox, had its last game that Saturday. His best friend, Tim, brought his trophy from the game to him that evening. I remember thinking that today was really the last baseball game.

Matt called in his two sisters to say goodbye. This was not the normal routine—Matt adored his sisters, but he never made a big deal of saying goodnight or goodbye. He also told his dad to cut down the apple tree in the backyard because it was diseased. I was confused. I didn't understand it at the time, but now I believe that Matt was making his final arrangements. He was tying up loose ends. He was worried and concerned about making sure things were done right and taken care of, I think, and I believe that Matt knew he was dying. He was not in pain, nor was he afraid—as far as we could tell. He was peaceful and matter-of-fact. Very Matt-like.

Those were the last words he spoke to us.

Everyone went home, but Rich and I. We both spent the night in Matt's room. The nurses told us he probably wouldn't make it through the night. We just took it one moment at a time, trusting God for strength each moment.

About 2:30 that morning, our nurse came in to wake us up. Matt's breathing had changed and she told us it was time to say goodbye....

Rich and I both went to his bedside and leaned down and told Matt that we loved him and we would see him in heaven. We watched as he took his last breath. He was so full of peace—I know that Jesus was there to take him to heaven.

We stayed in the room—we couldn't leave. I sat on the bed next to Matt and held his hand. I knew he wasn't there—it was just his body—but I held his hand anyway. I didn't want to let go.

Our pastor Jim and his wife Gail came to the hospital. They were there with us as they had been throughout our whole journey. They sat with us. We needed them there, and I know they knew that. No one said a word. We just sat together in Matt's room.

Dr. Clark also came by during the night and sat with us She didn't have to come—she had left all the necessary orders. We were thankful to see her.

About 6:30 in the morning, I suddenly noticed that Matt's hand was clammy and cold. There was no sign of life. It was time to go. I didn't want to leave Matt, even though I knew he was no longer occupying his body.

We walked outside that morning at 6:30 A.M. and the sky was blue and the day full of sunshine. Rich remarked that it seemed unfair to have such a beautiful day when our son had just died. Later, we would both realize that the sunshine was God saying to us that we would go on, and we would be okay.

Rich and I headed to Dwayne and Lorelle's house, where our girls were sleeping. I called the people I needed to call to tell them Matt was gone. I had prayed that Matt wouldn't die on Evie's birthday; she had walked with us through this whole journey. God answered my prayers. He died on June 7. I felt the urgency to call her—I spoke with her husband, Larry, to tell him Matt had died. I don't remember calling anyone else. I headed to bed and attempted to sleep.

Chapter 18

The Haze and Numbness Set In

"My flesh and my heart may fail,
But God is the strength of my heart,
my portion forever." Ps. 73:26

The next few days are a haze. I really don't recall what happened.

That evening after we left the hospital was a flurry of events.

My employer, Chuck Heffron, came by the house to see us. I was deeply touched.

I remember our friends Joe and Linda Sloss also coming to the house. Their son, John, was a close friend of Matt's.

I remember Matt's hamster, Fuzzball 2, biting Kristy that night. He had escaped from his cage—a normal event in our house—and was hiding under the couch. Little five-year-old Kristy tried to get him out and he had bitten her. We made a trip to the clinic that night to make sure she didn't need stitches. My dear friend Sandi was the nurse there that night. We didn't know each other well, yet—but she grew to be my close and treasured friend. Once again, I saw God's hand.

The next week continued to be a blur. Our dear daughter Aimee has since filled in so many spaces that I do not remember. I recall taking the girls to the funeral home to pick out Matt's casket—how bizarre that was. How do you pick out a casket for a little boy, let alone your son? Rich was much more practical. I was totally weirded out by the whole experience. I didn't want to be there, but knew it was necessary.

The next week was another fog of friends and family surrounding us with love, support, and encouragement. We were provided with meals and numerous offers of help; we had everything we needed.

Aimee and Kristy and I went shopping to pick out dresses to wear at Matt's memorial service. Aimee picked out a darling jumper in pink and blue and Kristy picked out a sweet dress in red with a Scottie dog on it. I went through the motions, but felt numb. I tried my best to provide some almost normal experiences for the girls.

Against my initial wishes, we did have a viewing for Matt. I had to learn that it was important for our family and friends to have an opportunity to say goodbye. My feelings were that I had already said goodbye and didn't feel the need to see his body anymore.

We picked out his clothes to be buried in. It only seemed fitting to choose his baseball uniform. Months later, Rich would show me the pictures of Matt in the casket. It wasn't Matt—he was gone.

6/9/1987-Maureen

Well, here we are six months plus after transplant—and Matthew's with the Lord. A mixture of feelings flood over me as I think back over the last 48 hours. Matt was so brave, but he suffered so the last week. He did not die in pain—at least it didn't seem so—he seemed so peaceful. Matt's lump on his neck was Burkitt's and he went through chemotherapy and radiation for 3 ½ weeks. Our doctor at the University of Washington, Steve Johnson, was super and caring. Matt still played Little League—he couldn't run because the Vincristine affected his joints—but he wouldn't let anyone run for him. He got to go to two Mariner's games—one for dinner where Mark Langston suited up and came in, even though he didn't play that night—it was his night off! He asked Matt whose autographs he wanted, and Matt asked for Spike Owens (on the Red Sox) and Alvin Davis. I'll never forget him sitting on the edge of his seat with his mitt on to catch a fly ball! The heme/onc clinic and Melanie, one of the Children's staff, arranged for Matt to throw out the opening pitch at the May 17 Mariner's game—he was so thrilled! May 8, they had found 540 Burkitt's cells in his spinal fluid (CSF) and he had facial paralysis and trouble swallowing—but that week at the hospital he improved and amazed the doctors! They had asked to make him a "no code," (order to not resuscitate if his heart stopped) because of the brain stem involvement, they thought—but Matt got better!

So, he went home Saturday, May 16, and threw out the pitch on May 17! He had double vision—but he did great!

Things were rough after that—Matt couldn't play, mostly because of his vision. But he just didn't feel like it—we prayed he would get better again, just like he did in the past. We started planning with him—camping at our lot over Memorial Day, going to see Gammy and Keith in June/July—Matt decided he wanted to be a doctor 'cuz they make lots of money. We did go camping over Memorial Day—he didn't feel very good. He started coming down with shingles on his chest—so he spent a lot of time by the fire and sleeping. He did river raft (with Uncle Mike because, "his Daddy didn't go through enough white water!") and then in the big raft—I still hear his voice and, "Yahoo, Yahoo!" as we hit the white water. We came home Memorial Day and Matt was really hurting. So, he was hospitalized just overnight to start Acyclovir for the shingles.

The next week was tough, because he started having so much pain—we thought it was due to the shingles. But that next Sunday night, every two-hour Demerol only lasted one hour and he was up all night. So, they hospitalized him (overnight hopefully) to get his pain under control. Matt must have known because he brought Melford and his pillow to the clinic appointment. Well, it turned out, Matt didn't come home—not to our home—he did go home to Jesus.

It is so hard and hurts so much even as I write this. His shingles pain had masked a lot of other symptoms. Pain in his arms and side—Rich noticed he couldn't lift his arms above his head and by Thursday/Friday—he couldn't turn his neck or keep his head up. Thursday the pain was gone, but other symptoms worsened. Thursday night while brushing his teeth, Matt fell off his chair and hit his head, and the Hickman line came out! So, #3 went in Friday night. The doctors waited until I could get there from work. How special. They did a bone marrow aspiration (during the surgery) and it was normal. Matt made sure—he asked Dr. Hickman to put the plastic clamps on! He came back from surgery asking for grape popsicles, cottage cheese, fruit cocktail, mashed potatoes, gravy, turkey, and dressing. He ate from 9:30 to midnight. He still would have continued except Mom got too tired.

The memorial service at our church was held on June 10. We met with our pastor and his wife, Jim and Gail, in the prayer room before the service. We prayed together, which I treasured. I was painfully hesitant to go into the church and face everyone. I'm not sure why I felt that way. Our little girls were there by our side every step of the way. How were they doing? My focus was only on me—I was so selfish looking back on that now. How were my little girls dealing with the loss of their brother?

We entered the church and were instantly overwhelmed. There were over five hundred people there in Matt's honor. I needed that. I needed to know that people wouldn't forget him. One of the speakers was Jennifer, Matt's best friend Tim's older sister. His Little League team sat in the front row, all in uniform. I was incredibly touched. Dr. Clark, his oncologist at Children's, spoke, as well as Otero Flower, our dear pediatrician who had diagnosed Matt. Our dear friend Marilyn sang the song Kristy had picked out—"This Is the Day that the Lord Has Made," and my favorite, "El Shaddai." It was an amazing service. I don't remember anything else.

I know we had a reception line in the church and I do remember some of the people coming through the line——but again, it is blurred.

There was a graveside service for Matt. Pastor Jim led it and asked people to share, who were standing around the grave. So many people shared precious moments from Matt's life—funny ones and touching ones. I treasured those in my heart and loved the intimate time with close friends and family.

Our family went home. What next? Every time I looked at Rich, I was reminded of the intense pain of our loss. It was hard to look at him. It made the hurt worse and more intense.

Aimee left for church camp the next day. People asked me, how could I let her go? I felt that it was important for her to go—to have that normal time with friends, and especially church friends. I prayed it was the right decision.

One week later, Rich's brother Gary was married. I see the pictures of us all at the wedding, but don't recall very much. I know we left the next day for Montana—the trip we had planned with Matt. It was hard to go, but we knew we needed to.

It was the beginning of a new start—a new start without Matt. I didn't know if I was ready—that years later I wouldn't be able to handle all the memories. We were blindly moving forward, one small step at a time, trusting that God would direct our paths.

And He did.

Chapter 19

The Grief Journey

"I will turn their mourning into joy; I will comfort
them, and give them gladness for sorrow."
Jeremiah 31:13

How do you go on after the death of a child? Without the Lord, I'm
not sure I would have gone on. I remember many times just
wanting to go to heaven and be with Matt. It was purely and
totally selfish—no thought of my husband or my girls or anyone
else. Those times were there, nonetheless. Life seemed too hard
to face. I was missing a part of me. I knew that as a mother, my
children were part of me. Now a part of me was forever missing
on this side of Heaven.

One of the hardest people to face was my husband. When I
looked at Rich and saw his pain, it hurt me even more. I couldn't
face more pain. I now understand why the divorce rate after the loss
of a child is 80%. We loved each other so much, but it was terribly
painful to see each other's grief. We couldn't talk about it; we
needed to present a strong front for our two little girls. It became
critical to find something to pull us back together.

Rich returned to full-time work and he would come home
exhausted—he had received a promotion just before Matt died. The
new position would require travel and much more responsibility. In
hindsight, I think it actually helped Rich, as it took so much

concentration and effort to work. It took his mind off the fact that his only son had died.

One night, a few months after Matt had died, he came home and asked me to take down all the pictures of Matt. I was devastated. I couldn't take them down. I hung on to all the pictures. My fear was that Matt would be forgotten. His pictures not only kept him close to me, but also showed me that he had lived. Rich told me that every picture he saw of Matt brought fresh pain, and he couldn't work with that pain. Rich graciously agreed to let me keep the pictures out.

A divorce rate of 80%. It was becoming clearer. We grieved so differently, Rich and I. I needed to talk about Matt all the time, and Rich needed to put the memory away, to compartmentalize it. We were growing farther and farther apart. Our only necessity was to survive.

Our head pastor of our church, Mark, suggested we attend a grief group. Neither one of us wanted to go. A grief group? Everyone sitting around crying? That was the last thing we were looking to do. However, we went. I will always remember turning the corner in the hallway of the church where it was held and hearing laughter. Rich and I both looked at each other. That can't be the grief group—they were laughing? What we found was a warm and welcoming group of people who understood us. They embraced us immediately and asked us to share our story. At last! I could talk! I had been feeling so badly, talking too much about Matt to anyone who would listen. They would end up crying and I'd feel terrible and guilty.

Rich and I shared Matt's journey and everyone patiently listened; some cried, some nodded their heads. Our facilitator, Margaret, was encouraging and empathetic. One by one, each member told their story—some were parents who had lost children to suicide or accidents. Others were friends or family members that had lost spouses or people close to them. All our stories were different, but we all knew the experience of loss. We talked about how to celebrate birthdays, Christmas, and special anniversaries. The group offered ideas on how to survive day by day and what helped and what didn't help.

Rich and I began to heal that night. We were beginning the grief journey, albeit differently, but together. I had hope once again that we could survive as a couple and a family, one moment at a time. I was back to the moment by moment survival, not taking on more than I could handle.

I mentioned earlier that Aimee had gone to a church camp scheduled soon after Matt's death. I had agonized over whether to let her go—would she be okay away from family so soon after her brother's death? Yet, I wanted her to know some normalcy. So we let her go for a week. I prayed that it was a good decision. She came home happy and told us she had a wonderful time. I believe the Lord was teaching me to let go a little bit at a time. My initial reaction was to gather both girls close to me and not let them out of my sight. My adult self reasoned that Aimee needed to know that I trusted her and God, and that she would be okay. It was the first of many times of letting go when I wanted so desperately to hold her close to me.

Aimee and Kristy's relationship as sisters was another story. Matt had always been a buffer between the girls—there was almost five years' difference in their ages. They really didn't interact very much—most of their interactions were with their brother. Now that buffer was gone. So, they fought, as sisters can do. I think, first of all, the age difference was a big reason. They were both in different stages of their lives—Kristy starting kindergarten and Aimee headed for junior high. Kristy wanted to be with Aimee all the time, and Aimee was striving fiercely for independence. I'm sure that she saw her as a pest at times, even though I know she loved her. Her focus was surviving adolescence and her friends. Kristy loved Aimee's attention and companionship. It hurt to see them so at odds, but I saw them work out their sibling relationship. I'm so proud of them.

I've wondered often how present Rich and I were for the girls. My absentmindedness, my own grief, and Rich and I going in different directions had to take a toll on our parenting. Friends stepped in on so many occasions and planned special things for Aimee and Kristy. Aimee flew to Texas to visit our former neighbors—that was another hard one for me to let go! Kristy grew to love Carol Kampman and Linda Sloss and their frequent trips to McDonald's for Happy Meals. Their two sons were some of Matt's best friends. I prayed we did a good job, but in the midst of grief, I understood we were on survival mode. We were blessed with amazing daughters. The more I look back, the more I realize that.

I can say I wanted—no, *longed*—to "do grief well." I know that sounds ridiculous even as I write those words. How do you do grief well? It is a messy, overwhelmingly difficult process. Now, I see that was an issue of pride. Outwardly, I thought it was the fact that I wanted to be a good witness to how God worked through this experience in our lives. I know that He did, but for some strange reason, I thought it was important for me to do grief well so that He didn't look bad. So much for my faulty theology! In reality, I think I wanted to make sure I did a good job, and so, get the credit for that. God deserves all the credit for carrying us through, day by day.

Going to church became difficult. Because we had been in front of the congregation sharing about Matt's healing and later his relapse, most people in our large church knew us. After Matt died, well-meaning people would come up to me and ask me how I was doing. Being the transparent person I am, I would tell them—good or bad. The conversation would usually be brief, with them crying and me talking way too much. We'd part with my feeling devastated and guilty that I had caused them pain. My response was twofold. Either I could choose to quit going to church, or when people asked me how I was doing, I could say "fine," or "as good as can be expected." I chose the latter. I believed they wanted to hear that I was okay, that's what they hoped to hear. It caused too much pain for me to share how I was really doing. It seemed totally contradictory, that at church, of all places, I couldn't be me. This was totally my own perception. People meant well and truly cared, but I couldn't handle their responses. So, I put on an outwardly appearing "brave front," a good smile, and lied my way through church. It was exhausting.

There were many people, dear friends, who accepted me and all my ugly emotions. They listened tirelessly, and I am amazed that they stayed by me through all this. Grief is ugly, painful, and exceedingly isolating. One can really only grieve alone. I had to work through this loss and the process was up to me to come out whole on the other side. Dear friends were patient with me, sat with me, and listened and listened and listened. They were present. Like Matt's friend Tim, who was present during the "yuckiest" times. Little notes of encouragement on our car windshield, cards, Bible verses jotted on scraps of paper and passed to us—these seemingly small presents were huge gifts and helped me move along the path of healing.

Chapter 20

Perspectives on Helping Grieving People from My Heart

"Therefore, since we are surrounded by so great a cloud of witnesses, let us run with endurance the race that is set before us..." Hebrews 12:1

As I shared in the introduction, my hope in writing this book was not only to honor Matt, but to also help families going through grief and those trying to love and care for them. People have often asked me what helped and didn't help during our journey of grief. My answers below are solely from my own perspective and experience, and are not meant to be the sum of all that is helpful or unhelpful for every family. I pray that these suggestions from our journey will be useful to some readers or their acquaintances.

Things not to say, please:
I understand how you're feeling.
I know what's it like.
If you'd only had more faith, he/she wouldn't have died.
God took Him to save him from (...) in the future.

You can have another child.

Be thankful you have other children.

You've grieved long enough. It's time to move on.

Grief should be over in six weeks (or enter any specific time).

People so often mean well, and long to say the "right thing" to ease your pain or make sense of your loss. I don't believe there is anything that can be said to accomplish this.

Helpful things to do and say:

I'm so sorry. Then hug them.

Listen to whatever they want to share and let them know it's okay if it makes them cry.

Don't say anything, just hold them and cry with them.

Be present. Sit with them. No words need to be spoken. Just your presence is comforting.

Send cards, words, memories of the one that was lost. These are so comforting to the family.

Accept them where they are in the grief process—don't place any expectations on them.

Provide practical helps without asking. Instead of saying, "What can I do to help?"—provide the help and allow them to accept or reject it (i.e., meals, housekeeping helps, gift certificates for time away or spa services like massages).

Invite them to dinners, movies, outings, but please understand if they say no. It may be too much right now, but maybe try again later.

Understand if they don't want to talk, take phone calls, participate in activities. For me, the phone was exhausting, because I had to share repeatedly the same story and often provide comfort for them.

When you visit, keep the visit short and be sensitive to body cues. The family is struggling to focus on the remaining children and time with them, yet at the same time be hospitable. One of my favorite gifts was when people would drop off meals or gifts at the door, but not come in. I was so appreciative of their sensitivity to be intact as a family and keep our focus there.

Remember the other children in the family. Small gifts, cards, remembrances for them go a long way to easing the grief. Speaking to them and hugging them, too, is critically important. Often the children get lost in the process, especially in the early days when chaos seems to reign.

Please allow the family to talk about their family member who died. It's healing and comforting for them. Try to be comfortable in their tears and pain. You don't have to say anything, just give them permission to talk about their loved one. Sometimes people fear if they bring him/her up, it will cause more pain. When allowed to talk about their loss, it provides healing.

Encourage the family members to journal as best you can. I rejected it initially, but now am so thankful I was "forced" to journal. I can look back at my grief journey and see even more clearly God's hand and presence along the way.

Most importantly, please pray for the family, not just initially but ongoing. God provides the healing along the grief journey.

Rich's letter for our Matt's memorial service: A Father's Perspective

As my only son, Matt and I long ago decided we had to stick together, since we were outnumbered by the girls in our family. Our Tonka trucks had to have equal space with the Barbie dolls. I enjoyed teaching him things that I thought he should know as he grew up. Riding a bike, catching and hitting a baseball, fishing, working on a car, wood-working, painting, gardening, and school work were just some of the things we shared. I really appreciated his desire to learn about the things I enjoyed. I watched with curiosity the development of his amazing mechanical abilities and Maureen often commented how she thought he would be an engineer someday like his dad. Our previous successful years as a family seemed to assure me of the years to come. It would continue to be fun comparing my ideas and dreams with the developing reality.

Then, nine months ago, I was jolted into facing the likelihood of Matt dying in a few months. My little half took the news so well. Could he comprehend what was going on? Where's God in all this? How am I supposed to deal with this? Urgent questions whose answers I knew would change all of our lives. In time and one by one, God would make sure all the questions were answered. But what about Matt and all his unspoken questions? How could I comfort him when I couldn't comfort myself? Looking back, now, I realize those things were taken care of. God really does protect, comfort, and cherish children. Over the weeks and months, I would discover that Matt already knew the answers to my questions.

First of all, with Jesus in our hearts, we had nothing to fear. Matt had complete trust in Jesus. I would find Matt's comfort by keeping focused on our guaranteed eternal life. I could no longer face the long range future plans I once cherished. I couldn't even plan the next few days. I felt that Matt surely couldn't comprehend the seriousness of the situation. He showed no sense of urgency and didn't worry about tomorrow. He just lived each day, one at a time. Another answer for me. And that answer would be driven home time and time again. You see, I didn't have the emotional strength for more than one day. I learned that during the long term crisis, God would start me out each day with just enough strength for that day. And when I jumped over today into tomorrow, I found the complexities to be more than I could effectively handle. As it was for Matt, the strength I needed always came, day by day, and every day. But what about God's plan—He can take any of us at any time, but would he let this disease cut Matt's time with us so short? Would He intervene? We prayed more than we ever have before and listened and watched for the responses. And they came! The initial remission, the transplant matches, many special experiences with Matt, the successful transplant itself, Matt home for Christmas, his 8th birthday, and unending care for us and our daughters, watching Matt enjoy all the attention and gifts, and so many more answers.

Yes, God was there. He intervened, and He answered our prayers. But the most significant answer came in January. Matt's leukemia had returned. It hadn't been eradicated and there was virtually no hope for him to live more than a few weeks.

But then the leukemia went away and stayed away, a miracle by all medical standards. We were overjoyed and so very thankful. But we couldn't overlook what God had just taught us. We didn't know God's plan for Matt or for any of us. We could thank Him for today and then hope for tomorrow, but most of all, we could trust Him and thank Him for being in control of all that happens to us.

God gave us six more months with Matt. Matt got to play baseball again, go to Mariner's games, go fishing, ride his new motorcycle, play with his GI Joe toys, go camping and river rafting, play with his friends, and be a normal boy again. We thanked God for each day and the special times.

I pray we won't forget the lessons God taught us through Matt. Aimee and Kristy and Maureen and I will miss him very much. But we will go on. God is still there and we will continue trusting Him. We will plan for the future, but more importantly, we will try to live each day to the fullest. We will trust our lives to God. I don't fear death so much anymore. I know that when God calls me, I will get to rejoin Matt.

I love you, Matt, and I hope you enjoy watching me grow up. I want to be just like you.

Your Dad

Epilogue

It has been almost thirty years to get this book from my mind and heart onto the printed page. My frustration has been that this has taken me so long to complete, but what I've found is that grief is a lifelong process. I'm not done with my grief journey, and I continue to learn more and more about what grief looks like.

My purpose for writing this book was first to honor Matt's legacy. It has always been important to me as a mom that he isn't forgotten. This book is my promise to Matt—that his life is remembered. It has also been a healing process to write his story. I've also learned that it has become important to me to honor my husband, Rich, and our two amazing daughters, Aimee and Kristy, and the way they have survived and how their own grief journey has taught me so much. I'm so proud to be part of this family.

The most important reason I write this book is to let you, my reader, know that God is trustworthy and sovereign. He loves us and is present throughout all the experiences of our lives. Without knowing the Lord and His peace and presence, I know I wouldn't have come through this journey whole. I know it would have probably destroyed me, my family, and those closest to us. He was my strength and peace, and more importantly, He was Matt's peace. Throughout his story, God's peace was evident in Matt's responses and actions. I want to share that, because it was both miraculous and comforting to me.

As I continue to walk this journey God has provided for me, I continue to see evidence of His fingerprints throughout my life. His fingerprints were evident in the small things we experienced through Matt's illness and treatments—Rich being there for the initial diagnosis, the lack of mucositis during transplant. I kept a journal of the miracles we experienced during that time, and they were numerous. Matt's healing in January was but one, but the many events I've described in his story were not coincidences. Rich and I both saw them as God being in control, carrying us each step of the way when we could not go on. His reassurance that He is sovereign are fingerprints on our lives and on my heart.

I have been asked over and over about how we survived losing our son. I can say without hesitation that it was through the Lord. My faith before was very surface level and small. Our journey with Matt and through the grief process has driven my faith deep in my heart, and I am so very thankful.